Contents

CW01669619

I Do Not See the Woman Hidden in the Forest: Surrealism and the Feminine

Alyce Mahon

René Magritte's composite work *Je ne vois pas la [femme] cachée dans la forêt* (*I do not see the [woman] hidden in the forest*, 1929) is often held up as an example of the 'problem' of woman in Surrealism. In it, a series of sixteen photographs of male Surrealists is staged around a photograph of a painting by Magritte himself, *La Femme cachée (The Hidden Woman)*. A nude woman forms the centre of the composition, and yet the portraits of the men that frame her all have their eyes closed – they do not *see* her.[1] She is staged as a figment of their erotic imaginations rather than flesh and bone. For Rudolf Kuenzli, this work by Magritte proves that male Surrealists 'did not see woman as subject, but as a projection, an object of their own dreams of femininity'; for Katharine Conley, it is a sign of male trepidation, 'They longed to discover Woman/Love in the woods but were ambivalent about actually reaching her and uncertain about their responses to them.'[2] Like the work of many other male Surrealists, Magritte's seems to buttress patriarchal society's objectification of woman, undermining the official stance of complete non-conformism and the laying waste to the ideas of family, country and religion as declared in the first and second manifestoes of 1924 and 1930 respectively. It seems to speak to a rhapsodic passage in the first manifesto, where we read: 'isn't what matters that we be masters of ourselves, the masters of women, and of love too?'[3]

Despite their ambition to revolutionise art and society, male Surrealists all too often held firm to a passive vision of woman which was indebted to 19th-century Romanticism and Symbolism. The idea of the (male) artist as a kind of knight-errant in pursuit of the (female) muse frequently emerges in their writings and images. Breton, for example, once wrote of a fantasy of pursuing the unknown and donning a gleaming suit of armour to 'recapture a little of the feeling of man of the 14th century'.[4] Thus while the centrality of love and desire to Surrealism undoubtedly brought gender to the forefront of artistic expression, the ideal of woman often inhibited Breton and his male comrades from initiating a radical revision of gender roles.[5] However, to read Surrealism in terms of master and muse alone is to interpret it too literally – we must recall that the Surrealist enterprise scrutinised desire and reality alike. Magritte and his Surrealist circle reveled in using words to negate images and using art to unsettle knowledge, implicating the reader/spectator in the process. His woman is 'hidden' in the sense that she is only a representation. As a title of one of his later paintings indicates, Magritte aimed to expose 'the universe unmasked' (*L'Univers démasqué*, 1932). In challenging representation itself in this manner, Surrealism exposed it as a social construct and, by extension, challenged patriarchal and masculinist rational norms. This critique opened a radical space for the feminine as the very antithesis of those traditional constructions and norms. Indeed, I would argue that Surrealism increasingly came to recognise that radical artistic and socio-political change could only find a new direction through the feminine. André Breton stated in his novel *Arcanum 17* (1944), written during the war while he was in exile in North America, 'the time has come to value the ideas of woman at the expense of those of man, whose bankruptcy is coming to pass fairly tumultuously today. It is artists, in particular, who must take the responsibility, if only to protest against this scandalous state of affairs, to maximize the importance of everything that stands out in the feminine world view in contrast to the masculine, to build only on woman's resources.'[6] World war re-ignited their focus on woman – as Simone de Beauvoir astutely observed in *The Second Sex* (1949): 'Breton venerates woman because she brings peace'.[7]

Women artists began to join the movement just before the war and seized the feminine for their own artistic expression, expanding the boundaries of Surrealist imagery and ideology in the process. The English-born Surrealist Leonora Carrington insisted all knowledge, if not the Holy Grail itself, ended in woman. Carrington recounted in her memoir, *Down Below* (1944), which documents her experience of mental collapse and hospitalisation in a Spanish asylum in war-torn Europe: 'I was she who revealed religions and bore on her shoulders the freedom and the sins of the earth changed into Knowledge, the

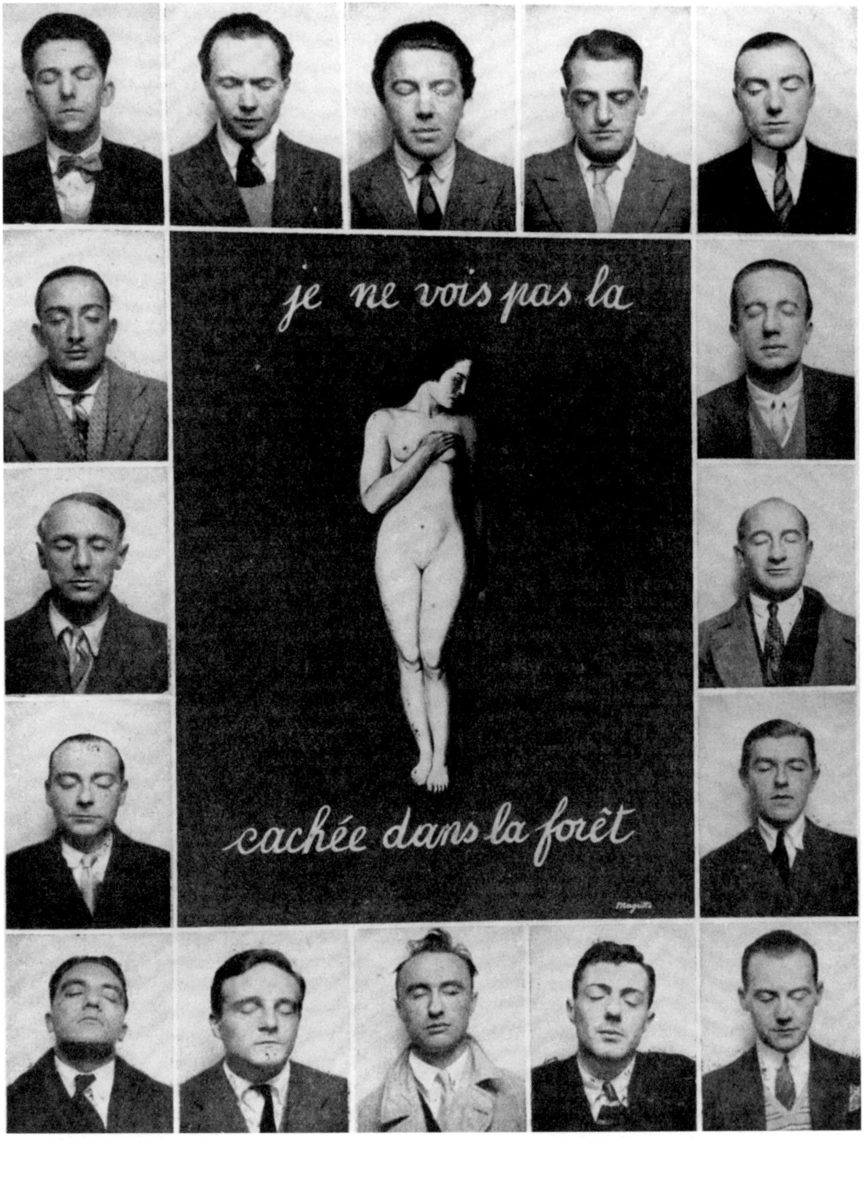

René Magritte
***Je ne vois pas la [femme] cachée dans la forêt*, 1929**
Photomontage for *La Révolution Surréaliste*

4

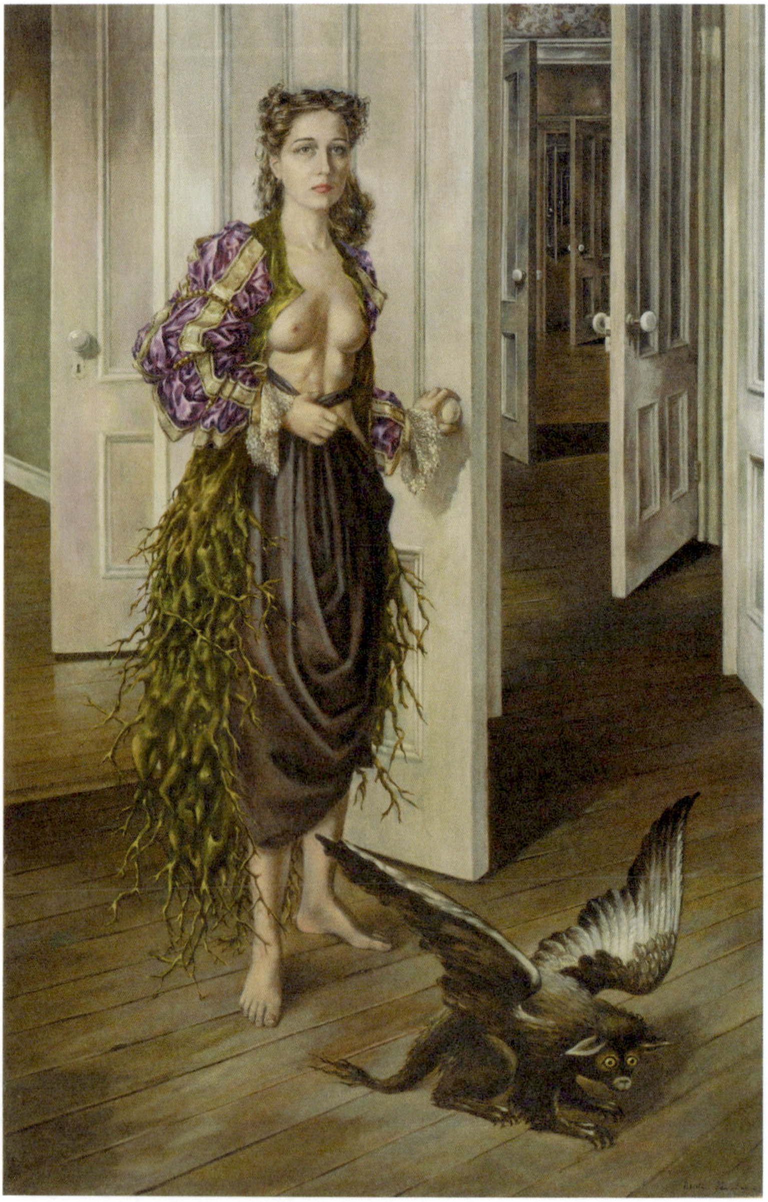

Dorothea Tanning
***Birthday*, 1942**
Oil on canvas, 102.2 x 64.7 cm

union of Man and Woman with God and the Cosmos, all equal between them.'[8] This spirit informs her painting of the same name, *Down Below* (1943), in which we find a procession of feminine archetypes (sphinx, harlot, goddess), as well as a self-portrait and a triumphal horse, all staged in unison in nature. Carrington shows female ancestors leading her out of the personal and political horror of war.

Women Surrealists' interest in feminine archetypes often entailed a focus on the young girl or '*femme-enfant*', the seductive or castrating 'goddess', or the old crone with all her magical skill. Such roles emerged in the self-portrait, as in *Birthday* (1942), by the American Surrealist Dorothea Tanning, in which she portrays herself defiantly staring out of the frame in a domestic interior with many open doors. Her bare breasts and Shakespearean costume with writhing erotic bodies and roots in its silken folds, as well as the chimerical creature at her feet, suggest her seductive and magical powers. This painting was selected by Max Ernst for Peggy Guggenheim's exhibition '31 Women' in her Art of this Century Gallery in New York in 1943. It was also reproduced in the Surrealist review *VVV* (nos.2–3, March 1943) alongside Tanning's short story 'Blind Date'. An absurdist tale involving a young woman and sewing machine, this story spoke of a physical and spiritual 'threshold' – a metaphor of rebirth often symbolised by the open doorway in Tanning's oeuvre: 'Tremble a little upon the threshold [...] Today you have been born out of abysmal sorrow [...] out of hates and holocausts, frenzy crimes, visions, scorpions, secretions, love and the devil. Today you shall be married to your future.'[9]

The sphinx-like female in *Le Bout du Monde* (*The Ends of the Earth*, 1948) by the Argentine-an-born Surrealist Leonor Fini, also reinforces this potent vision of the feminine. As Fini explained: 'She is woman, symbol of beauty and deep knowledge [...] the essential element of life, the primeval material, because she knows how to survive the cataclysm.'[10]

Reared in Trieste, Fini was a self-taught artist who mainly took inspiration from the Old Masters, reworking a traditional mythological iconography into a surreal one. She travelled to Paris in 1931 and by 1936 was exhibiting alongside the Surrealists there; whilst she spent the war years in Italy she also featured in Guggenheim's '31 Women' show alongside Carrington and Tanning.

Guggenheim's exhibition of contemporary women artists in 1943 reminds us of how pioneering this generation was and the challenges they faced as they demanded to be recognised as artists proper. As one critic observed of the show, 'The women – they could never be laughingly referred to as ladies – present a chinkless armoured front.'[11] And yet many women Surrealists resisted group exhibitions and studies of their art as 'women' after the war and throughout their long careers. For example, Fini

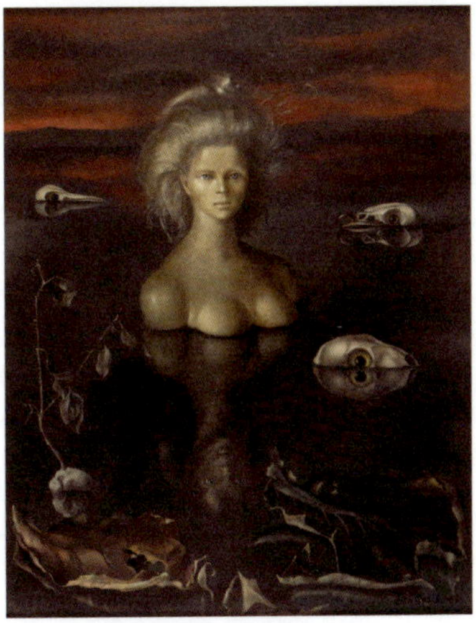

Leonor Fini
***Le Bout du Monde*, 1948**
Oil on canvas, 34.9 x 27.9 cm

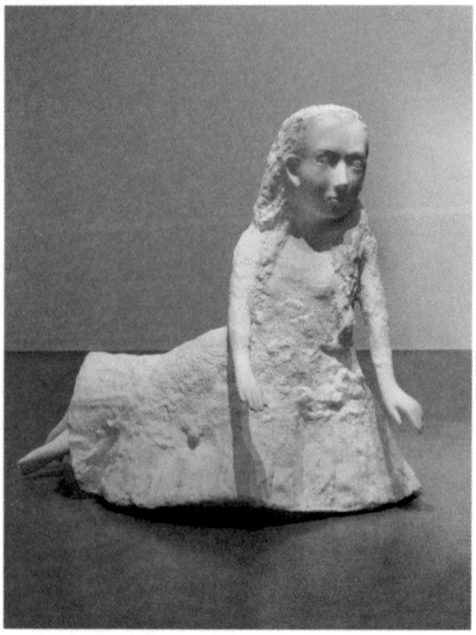

Kiki Smith
***Seer (Alice I)*, 2005**
White auto body paint on bronze
158.8 x 141 x 124.5 cm

regretted her contribution to Whitney Chadwick's ground-breaking publication *Women Surrealists* (1985), explaining in a letter to Chadwick: 'Men have tried to exile, to imprison, women. A study exclusively devoted to women is still a sort of exile.'[12] Tanning also resisted any essentialist reading of her art, once stating: 'Women artists. There is no such thing – or person. It's just as much a contradiction in terms as "man artist" or "elephant artist". You may be a woman and you may be an artist; but the one is a given and the other is you.'[13]

Women Surrealists are best viewed as exemplary of the 'new woman' of the interwar period, many of whom sought out the Paris of Surrealism from across the globe and all of whom rejected traditional gender roles in the process. As Shari Benstock documents in *Women of the Left Bank: Paris, 1900–1940* (1986), Paris was unique in offering that generation a space and community to deconstruct and reconstruct what it meant to be a woman.[14] Later, with the outbreak of World War II and exile of Breton and many Surrealists to New York, the influence of Surrealism on younger American artists extended there too. Surrealism offered a powerful and universal means to women to master their own image. It led them to challenge stereotypes, to advance the 'lesser' feminine genres of the still life, landscape and self-portrait, and to refashion the domestic object in art, so that the private and public, personal and political, became inextricable. It led them to answer back to Sigmund Freud's patriarchal view of 'the sexual life of grown-up women [as a] "dark continent" for psychology' with a new iconography of fear and fantasy.[15] And, by and large, and despite working from Paris to Prague, London and New York, they mapped out this new frontier on the female body – and, given their preference for self-portraits, often on their own womanly form.

Thus, while it would be essentialist and erroneous to try to force a common style or perspective on women Surrealists' art, given their obsessive return to the female body and sexuality we can recognise many common themes in their work. They turned to mythology to ensure matriarchal stories were not lost. They gave voice to feminine *jouissance*, teasing out woman's erotic pleasure and humour. They gave a voice to the 'Self' and yet staged their personal lives in such a way as to have a universal symbolism, most typically in forging an alliance between woman, alchemy, spirituality and Mother Nature. Moreover, many of these themes overlap in their art. In Ithell Colquhoun's small *Tree Anatomy* (1942), the mythological motif of woman as arboreal figure is seized to fashion a powerful, sexually assertive image of creativity, if not the origin of the world itself. Colquhoun presented what she and fellow Surrealists termed a 'psychological morphology' in the process, so that form reflects a state of mind, or 'inscape'.[16]

7

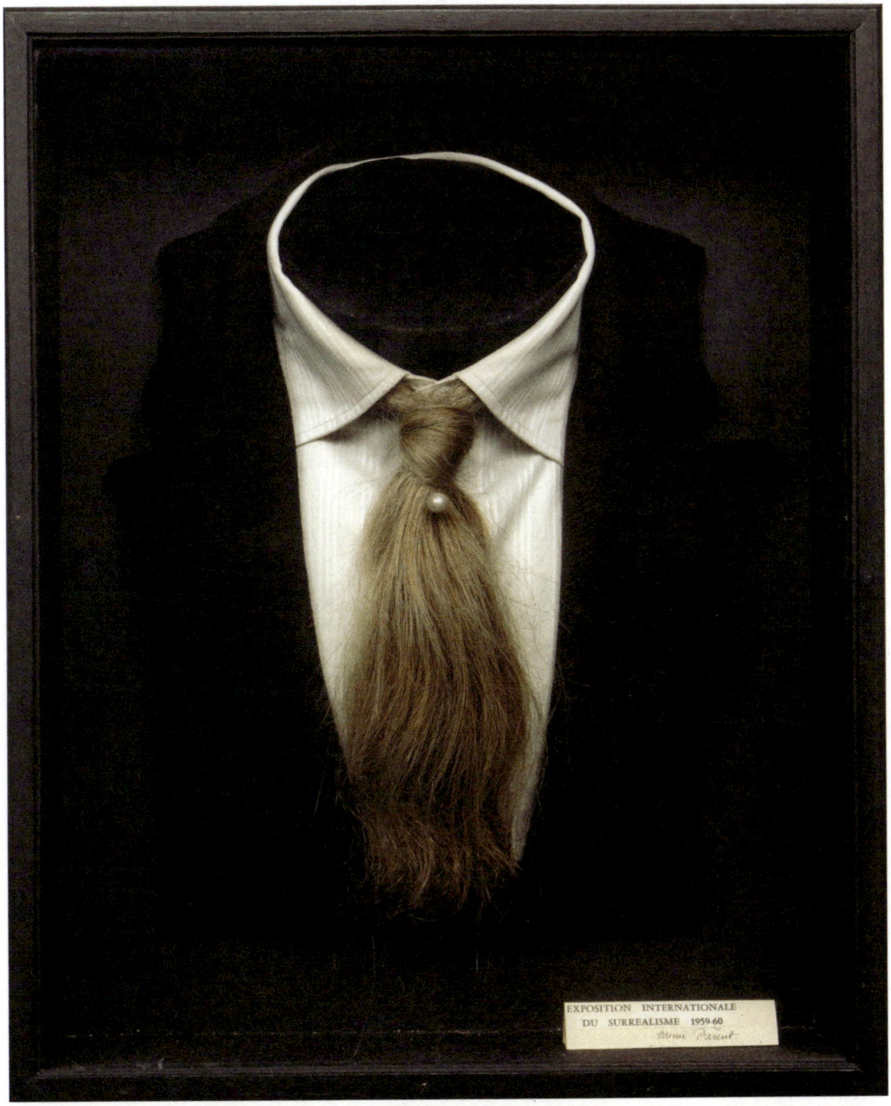

Mimi Parent
***Masculin/Féminin*,1959**
Jacket, shirt, hair and tie pin, 47.5 x 38 x 12.2 cm

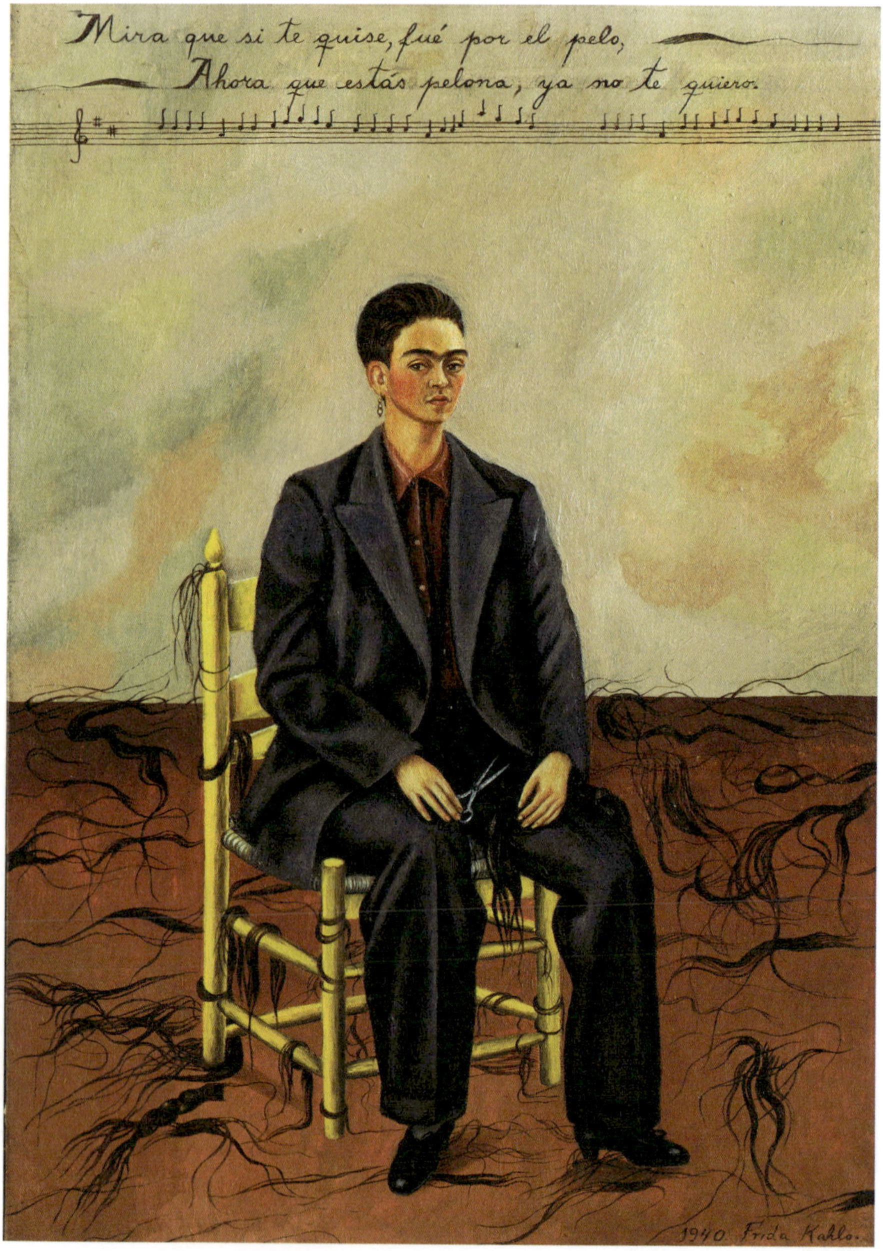

Frida Kahlo
***Self-Portrait with Cropped Hair*, 1940**
Oil on Canvas, 40 x 27.9 cm

Colquhoun's art looked to British and French Surrealism: in 1939 she had a joint exhibition with Roland Penrose at the Mayor Gallery, London, and the same year visited Paris, meeting the Surrealist circle there. However, where Breton grew increasingly interested in magic during the war and promoted it in the first post-war international Surrealist exhibition in Paris in 1947, Colquhoun's obsession with occultism led to her expulsion from the London Surrealist group in 1940. Thereafter, she became further immersed in English occult circles: in the 1950s she joined Aleister Crowley's Ordo Templi Orientis and Kenneth Grant's New Isis Lodge, and in 1961 she was ordained a deaconess in the Saint Église Celtique en Bretagne, the Ancient Celtic Church. It is this fusion of Surrealism and Celticism which emerges in her art and writings, advancing what has been described as an 'esoteric feminism' in Surrealism.[17]

The focus on feminine archetypes by women Surrealists such as Carrington, Tanning, Fini and Colquhoun, paved the way for later generations of feminist art. For example, Kiki Smith's Seer *(Alice I)* (2005) exemplifies her career-long revision of female archetypes in popular and mythological stories, from Little Red Riding Hood to the Medusa.[18] Surrealists looked to Lewis Carroll's *Alice's Adventures in Wonderland* (1865) and *Through the Looking Glass and What Alice Found There* (1869) as exemplary of a world 'the other side of the mirror'. Tanning's oil painting *Eine Kleine Nachtmusik* (1943) stages two Alice-like girls in a state of somnambulist ecstasy as indicated by their electrified hair and ripped clothing. The writhing, gargantuan sunflower and series of doors – including one that is open and beckoning with golden light – reinforce the girls' boldness, or even terrifying curiosity, in the face of the unknown. Smith's *Alice* alludes to the Surrealists' rendition of Alice as a *femme-enfant*, the pre-pubescent girl who not only embodies a precocious sexuality and supernatural force but who tries to lure the spectator into a Wonderland. The figure of Alice highlights another dominant theme in women Surrealists' work – *érotisme noir* – where the active, fatal or even Sadean potential of female erotic desire was harnessed. Canadian Surrealist Mimi Parent's object-tableau of 1959, *Masculin/Féminin* is a wonderful example of what Xavière Gauthier, in her study *Surréalisme et sexualité* (1971), lauds as '*femellitude*'. Gauthier used this term to explain that women Surrealists engaged with female sexuality in terms which were just as explicit as those used by male artists, that they refused to view woman as a 'facile complement' or 'weak negative' of male sexuality.[19] In *Masculin/Féminin*, a photograph of which the Surrealists used to advertise their 1959 international exhibition dedicated to Eros, Parent made a tie from her own blonde hair and set it against a man's white

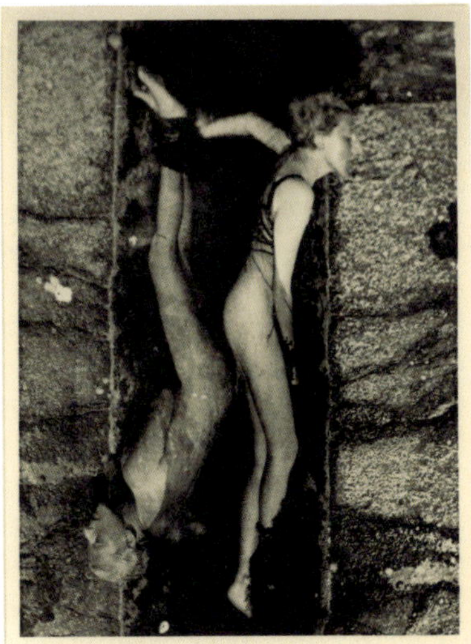

Claude Cahun
***Self-Portrait (double exposure in rock pool)*, 1928**
12.7 x 17.6 cm

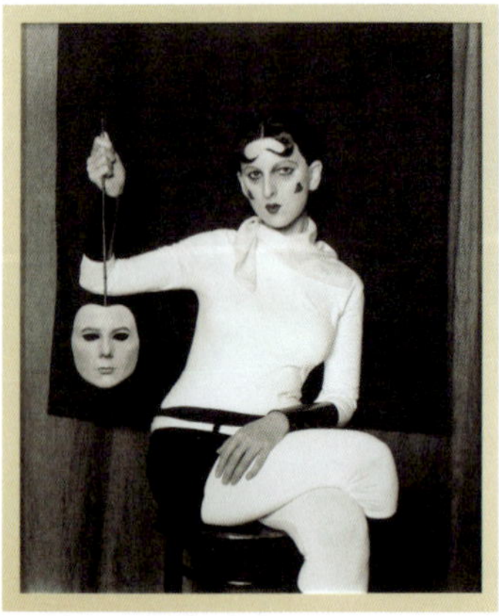

Gillian Wearing
***Me As Cahun Holding A Mask Of My Face*, 2012**
Bromide Print, 157.3 x 129 cm (framed)

shirt and suit lapels, its knot held in place with a pearl pin. Female hair is typically prized as a sign and symbol of fecundity and unfettered desire or seduction (especially when let loose, untied). In fashioning her long locks into a quintessentially male item of clothing, therefore, Parent queered gender norms, enjoying the fetish for, and tactility of, body hair. *Masculin/Féminin* also has an element of aggression, the 'scalped' hair suggesting the symbolic threat of castration.

It brings to mind Frida Kahlo's *Self-Portrait with Cropped Hair* (1940), in which she portrayed herself seated in an oversized man's suit, yielding a pair of scissors close to her sex, her long hair cut off in chunks that writhe around her like tendrils. In her painting, Kahlo included the words of a popular Mexican love song in the composition: 'Mira que si te quise, fué por el pelo, Ahora que estás pelona, ya no te quiero' (See, if I loved you, it was for your hair, now you're bald, I don't love you anymore). *Self-Portrait with Cropped Hair* was painted soon after Kahlo divorced Diego Rivera, whose infidelities included an affair with her younger sister Cristina – on learning of that affair Kahlo cut her hair boyishly short.

The art of Parent and Kahlo further exemplifies women Surrealists' obsessive use of fetishistic objects or materials (hair, stockings, gloves, velvet and fur) to empower the female Self and queer desire, as well as their irreverent playful dare to the spectator to 'please touch'.[20] Their Freudian play presaged the subversive sexual forms of Hannah Wilke's *Five Androgynous and Vaginal Sculptures* (1960–61), the animation of the inanimate domestic object in Laurie Simmons, *Magnum Opus II (The Bye-Bye)* (1991) or *Walking Cake II* (*Color*) (1989), and the crafting of beads from strands of her own hair by Mona Hatoum in *Hair Necklace* (2013). Women Surrealists' use of photography to explore gender as performance was equally ground-breaking. As in her *Self-portrait (double exposure in rock pool)* (1928), Claude Cahun frequently used the motif of doubling to produce formless silhouettes which dismantled sexual norms, whether through double exposure or the use of a mirror as prop. In so doing, Cahun undermined Freud's reading of same-sex desire as a sign of narcissism and played with the subversive potential of camouflage by merging woman's body with nature.[21] In her semi-autobiographical work *Aveux non Avenus* (*DisAvowals* or *Cancelled Confessions*, 1930), Cahun traced an interior journey through a mix of poems, essays and photomontages, writing on one image: 'Sous ce masque un autre masque. Je n'en finirai pas de soulever tous ces visages' (Under this mask, another mask. I will never finish removing all these faces). Here she anticipated contemporary women artists' 'acting out' of stereotypical gender roles – indeed, Gillian Wearing acknowledged her debt to Cahun in *Me as Cahun Holding a Mask of My Face* (2012).[22]

We find traces of Cahun's aesthetic in the art of Francesca Woodman too, especially that open spirit of self-discovery, formal experimentation, and determination to make the familiar strange. There seems to be nostalgia for an earlier form of photography not only in Woodman's choice of black-and-white film and use

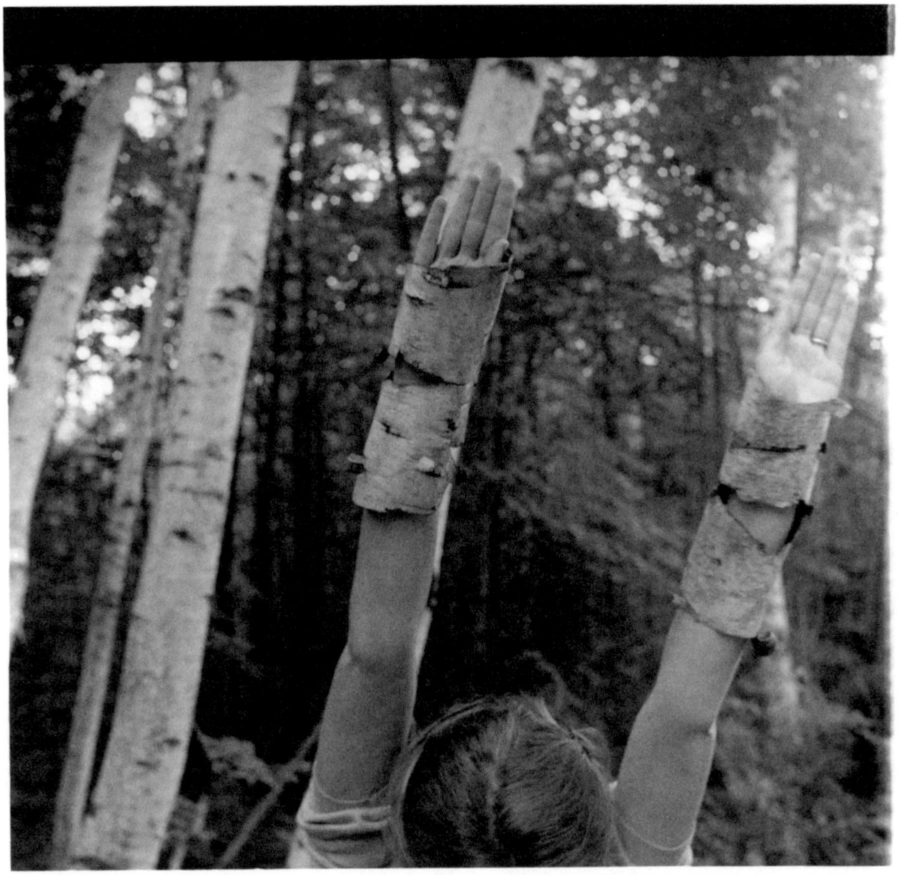

Francesca Woodman
Untitled (MacDowell Colony, Peterborough, New Hampshire), 1980
Gelatin silver estate print, 20.3 x 25.4 cm

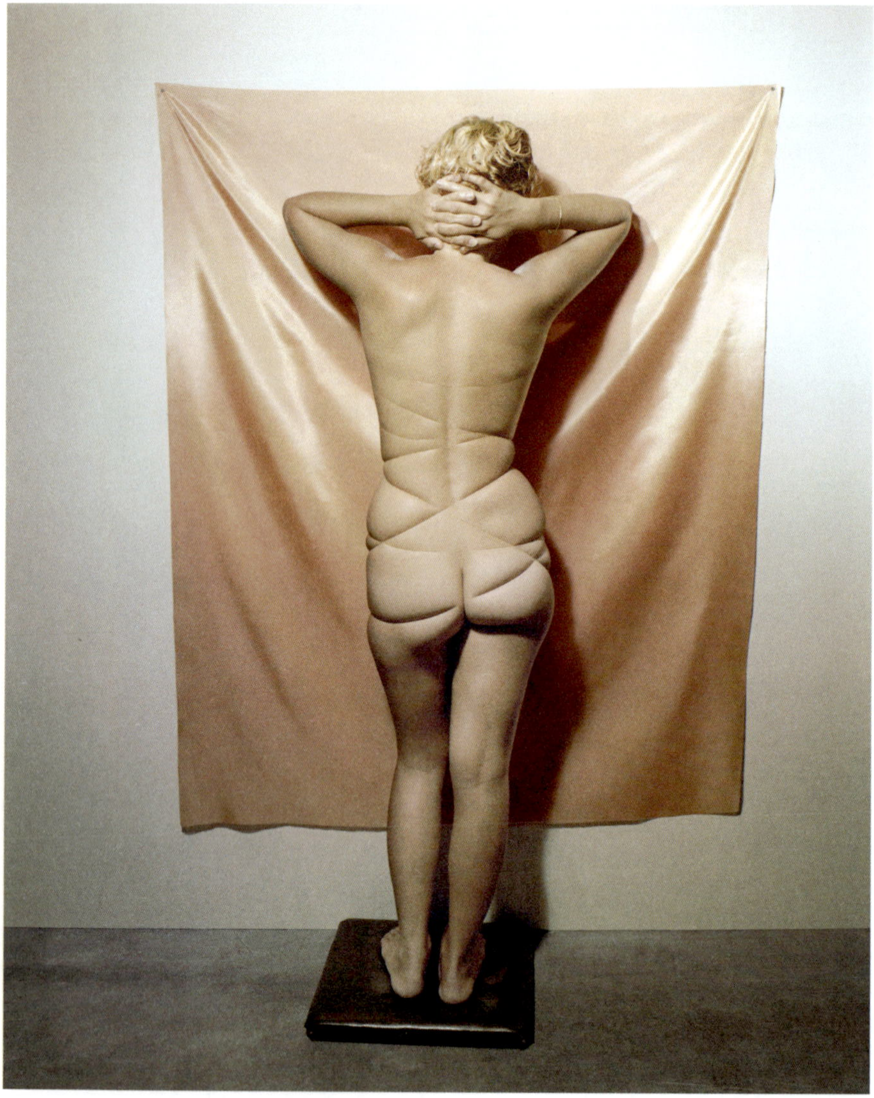

Jo Ann Callis
Untitled (Tied up), c.1976, From *Early Color Portfolio*
Archival pigment print, 40.6 x 50.8 cm

of long-exposure but in the attention to recognisable Surrealist motifs such as hands, mirrors and shadows. In *Untitled (MacDowell Colony, Peterborough, New Hampshire)*, 1980, Woodman uses photography to stage the female form and trees, flesh and bark, as one – a clever twist on '*la femme cachée dans la forêt*'. The spectator questions seeing and knowing, but at the same time the allegiance between woman and nature, mythology and creativity, is still evoked. We might think of the mythological tale of Daphne fleeing the desiring Apollo – she changes into a laurel tree to save her virtue – or of Colquhoun's *Tree Anatomy* (1942), or of Cahun's use of camouflage.

Other contemporary women artists seem to look to Hans Bellmer's handmade dolls of 1934–36, or his less well known but equally disturbing series of photographs *Unica Ligotée* (1958), where he frames his lover, the artist Unica Zürn, like a joint of meat bound in string. In such works, as Bellmer explained, he treated the female form as 'a sentence that invites us to rearrange it'; underpinning this surgical assault was his ambition to make visible what people refuse to see – from sexual taboo to the body politic of Nazi Germany.[23] Jo Ann Callis *Untitled* (1976), from her *Early Color Portfolio*, also lingers over the imprint of binds on bare skin, as Bellmer did in his portraits of Zürn. And yet, where the clinical documentary mood of Bellmer's intimate images is augmented by his black- and-white film, a kitsch commercial quality emerges in Callis' use of colour and props. She continues Cahun and Bellmer's use of photography as fabrication, challenging its 'truthful' status in highly staged images. One might also draw *It's The Buzz, Cock!* (2015) by Linder into this strand of Neo-Surrealism given that she also collages and 'rearranges' the body into uncanny, provocative forms. The work originates in her cover design for the 1977 single *Orgasm Addict* by the Manchester band the Buzzcocks, and it offers a punk assault on the art canon in recalling the brutal sexism of Magritte's oil painting *Le Viol* (*The Rape*, 1934), where he literally projected male desire onto the female by morphing her genitals into her face. With postmodern irony, however, Linder takes Magritte's oft-cited ambition to make the everyday 'shriek aloud' in a bold new feminist direction, and with an irreverence that many women Surrealists would have enjoyed.[24]

Many contemporary women artists frequently display or acknowledge a debt to Surrealists and especially to Surrealist women. Like their predecessors, they consistently ask us to look at the world through new eyes: our attention is drawn to the marvellous in the everyday, to matriarchal tales rather than patriarchal ones, to the erotic touch rather than the erotic gaze, and to the vital need to map identity in all its multiplicity. In both eras, around World War II and in more recent times, we not only find the emergence of the 'hidden' woman in their art but see her afresh, liberated and laughing. Representation is politicised, traditional aesthetic disinterestedness is done away with, and the Surrealist ambition to revolutionise desire and overthrow traditional values is channelled into radical new means of self-expression. This is surely where Surrealism's voice is most powerful and why its legacy continues to be relevant today.

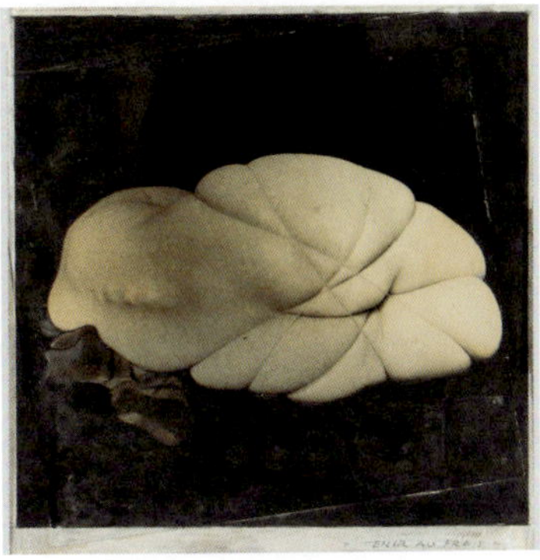

Hans Bellmer
***Tenir au Frais*, 1958**
Collage of vintage gelatin silver print and gouache on Masonite, 23.4 x 23.9 cm
Ubu Gallery, New York

14

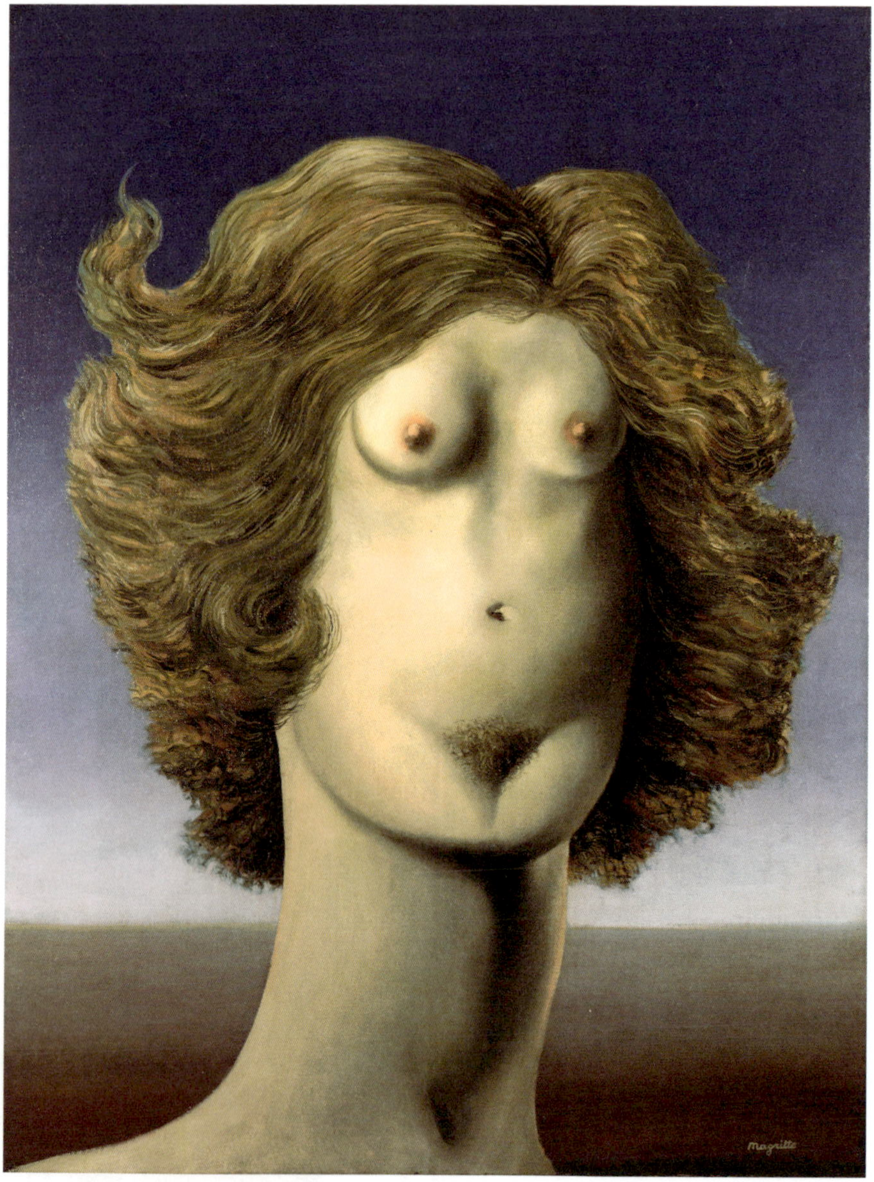

René Magritte
***Le Viol*, 1934**
Oil on canvas, 73.3 x 54.6 cm

1. The image was published on the back cover of the Surrealist journal *La Révolution surréaliste*, no.12, 15 December 1929. This edition included a questionnaire on love (and fifty-three responses by Surrealists) as indicated by the headline on its cover, 'Quelle sorte d'espoir mettez-vous dans l'amour?'

2. Rudolf Kuenzli, 'Surrealism and Misogyny' in Mary Ann Caws, Rudolf Kuenzli and Gwen Raaberg (eds.), *Surrealism and Women*, MIT Press, Massachusetts, 1991, p.18; Katharine Conley, *Automatic Woman: The Representation of Woman in Surrealism* University of Nebraska Press, Lincoln and London, 1996, p.17.

3. André Breton, 'Manifesto of Surrealism' (1924) in *Manifestoes of Surrealism*, trans. Richard Seaver and Helen R. Lane, Ann Arbor Paperbacks, University of Michigan Press, Michigan, 1972, p.17.

4. André Breton, 'Discours sur le peu de réalité' ('Introduction to the Discourse on the Paucity of Reality', 1924), in Breton, *What is Surrealism?: Selected Writings*, ed. Franklin Rosemont, Pathfinder, New York, 1978, pp.17–28, p.17.

5. See Whitney Chadwick, *Women Artists and the Surrealist Movement*, Thames & Hudson, London, 1985, p.31.

6. André Breton, *Arcanum 17* (1945), trans. Zack Rogow, Sun & Moon Press, Los Angeles, 1994, p.61.

7. Simone de Beauvoir, *The Second Sex* (1949), trans. Constance Borde and Sheila Malovany-Chevallier, Jonathan Cape, London, 2009, p.271.

8. Leonora Carrington, *Down Below* (1944) anthologised in *The House of Fear: Notes from Down Below*, Virago Books, London, 1989, p.195. See also Alyce Mahon, 'She Who Revealed: The Celtic Goddess in the Art of Leonora Carrington', in Sean Kissane (ed.), *Leonora Carrington*, Irish Museum of Modern Art, Dublin and D.A.P., New York, 2013, pp.126–153.

9. Dorothea Tanning, 'Blind Date', *VVV*, nos.2–3, March 1943, p.104.

10. Leonor Fini in interview with Peter Webb, Paris, 21 May 1993, cited in Peter Webb, *Sphinx: The Art and Life of Leonor Fini*, Vendome Books, New York, 2009, p.143. See also Alyce Mahon, 'La Feminité Triomphante: Leonor Fini and the Sphinx', *Dada/Surrealism*, Special Issue: 'Wonderful Things: Surrealism and Egypt', vol.19 no.1, December 2013 (http://ir.uiowa.edu/dadasur/vol19/iss1/10/).

11. R.F., '31 Odd Women at Peggy Guggenheim's', *Art News*, 1 February 1943, p.20.

12. Chadwick, p.236.

13. Carlo McCormick, 'Interview with Dorothea Tanning', *BOMB*, no.33, Fall 1990, pp.36–41

14. Shari Benstock, *Women of the Left Bank: Paris, 1900–1940*, Virago Press, London, 1986, pp.405–06.

15. Sigmund Freud, 'The Question of Lay Analysis. An Introduction to Psycho-Analysis' (1926), trans. Nancy Procter-Gregg, Imago Publishing Company Ltd., London, 1947, p.35.

16. The Chilean Surrealist Roberto Matta (1911–2002), whom Colquhoun met in Paris in 1939, first coined this term in 1938–39 to denote 'inscapes' or psychological landscapes.

17. In *The Goose of Hermogenes* (1961), a hermetic novel which was largely written in the early 1940s, Colquhoun again explores a comparable potent relationship between woman and land, occultism and the feminine. On esoteric feminism in Surrealism, see Janice Hellend, "Surrealism and Esoteric Feminism in the Paintings of Leonora Carrington", *Revue d'art candienne*, vol.16, no.1, 1989, pp.53–61 and Victoria Ferentinou, 'Ithell Colquhoun, Surrealism and the Occult', *Papers of Surrealism*, no.9, Summer 2011(http://www.surrealismcentre.ac.uk/papers ofsurrealism/journal9/index.htm).

18. See Marina Warner, 'Wolf-girl, Soul-bird: The Mortal Art of Kiki Smith', in *Kiki Smith: A Gathering, 1980–2005*, Walker Art Center, Minneapolis, 2005, pp.42–53.

19. Xavière Gauthier, *Surréalisme et sexualité*, Gallimard, Paris, 1971, p.275.

20. *Prière de toucher (Please touch)* was the title of the 1947 International Surrealist Exhibition catalogue, produced by the Galerie Maeght, Paris. The *edition de luxe* was designed by Marcel Duchamp and Enrico Donati and had a false rubber breast on a piece of black velvet on the front, and a label with this instruction on the back.

21. In his 1910 study of Leonardo da Vinci, Freud discusses his homosexuality in light of 'revivals of himself in childhood [...]. He finds the objects of his love along the path of narcissism, as we say.' The essay was translated into French in 1927 and would have been familiar to Cahun and her fellow Surrealists. Sigmund Freud, 'Leonardo da Vinci and a Memory of his Childhood', *Pelican Freud Library, Vol.14: Art and Literature*, trans. James Strachey, Pelican Books, Harmondsworth,1985, pp.151–231, p.191.

22. See Sarah Howgate and Dawn Ades, *Gillian Wearing and Claude Cahun: Behind the Mask Another Mask*, National Portrait Gallery, London, 2017.

23. Hans Bellmer in interview with Peter Webb, Paris, 15 January 1972, cited in Peter Webb, *The Erotic Arts*, Secker and Warburg, London, 1975; 1983 edn., p.370. See also Alyce Mahon, 'Hans Bellmer's Libidinal Politics' in *Surrealism, Politics and Culture*, Raymond Spiteri ed. and Donald LaCoss, Ashgate, Aldershot, 2003, pp.246–66.

24. Gisèle Ollinger-Zinque and Frederik Leen (eds.), *Magritte, 1898–1967*, Royal Museum of Fine Arts of Belgium, Brussels and Ludion Press, Ghent, 1998, p.21.

The Form of the Flower is Unknown to the Seed

Susanna Greeves

Woman has a powerful presence in Surrealism. She is the object of masculine desire and fantasy; a harpy, goddess or sphinx; a mystery or threat. She embodies the idealised feminine qualities of the irrational and unconscious, and thus serves as a medium for true surreality. Often, she appears decapitated, distorted, trussed up. Fearsome or fetishised, she is always the 'other'. From today's perspective, gender politics can seem the unlikely blind spot of a movement that declared war on patriarchal society, convention and conformity. Nonetheless, from the earliest days of Surrealism, female artists have been drawn to its emphasis on personal and artistic freedoms and to the creative potential that the exploration of the unconscious offered. By focusing on the work of women artists, 'Dreamers Awake' hopes to show how, through art anchored in corporeality, the symbolic woman of Surrealism is refigured as a creative, sentient, thinking being.

Represented here are some of the many women with important, though sometimes complicated, relationships to the historical movement, including Lee Miller, often categorised as muse or mistress; Leonora Carrington, who removed herself to Mexico to develop her work in isolation; Leonor Fini, who showed with the Surrealists but was not counted among them; and, as well as Eileen Agar, a company of lesser-known British Surrealists. Alongside them, some key figures in the development of contemporary art, including Hannah Wilke, Louise Bourgeois, Rosemarie Trockel, Kiki Smith, Mona Hatoum, Tracey Emin and Sarah Lucas, testify to the far-reaching influence of Surrealism through the intervening decades. Today, one hundred years since Apollinaire coined the term '*surrealisme*', certain visual tropes of Surrealism have long permeated popular culture, the unconscious mind is familiar territory, and the word 'surreal' itself debased to the point of meaninglessness, a word to reach for when the world around us bears a resemblance to reality but has taken on nightmarish qualities – the trending word, no less, of the past year of extremes.[1] Nevertheless, in our contemporary era so preoccupied with the politics of identity, we see the renewed relevance of Surrealism's strategies and ideas: in particular to a younger generation of artists, perhaps newly woken to an age of social conservatism where women's bodies are again a battleground, and the advances of previous generations must be continually defended.

This is a story told through the body, both defining it and transcending it. The fragmented, headless body of surrealism, repossessed by its owner, is wielded with all the power of the fetish; used ironically, subverting the objectifying gaze, or made a vehicle for self-expression. Object becoming subject, the artist is relocated inside the body, exploring its capacity for both suffering and pleasure, and expanding the amorphous, tactile possibilities of sculpture. The boundaries of the body are transcended in physical terms, exposing the workings of the hermetic body, and in metaphysical terms, shedding light on Freud's 'dark continent' of female sexuality. Identity and outward appearance are represented as fluid or changeable, celebrated as a plurality of selves to be assumed in a process of continual transformation. In her autobiography, reflecting on Surrealism's evolution, the British Surrealist Eileen Agar wrote that 'the form of the flower is unknown to the seed'.[2] The seeds to be found in the enormously fertile avant-garde of Surrealism have flourished in ways unforeseen by the movement's founders, and we see their tendrils surface in post-minimal sculpture, pop, punk and recent figurative painting, making surprising connections across subsequent generations of women artists.

‘Headless. And also footless. Often armless too: and always unarmed, except with poetry and passion. There they are, the surrealist women so shot and painted, so stressed and dismembered, punctured and severed: is it any wonder she has (we have) gone to pieces?’ [3]

Such is Mary Ann Caws' charge against the male Surrealists. Shown here echoing the images of Hans Bellmer's disturbing dolls, or Man Ray's particular fascination with Lee Miller's torso, are more headless, faceless forms, by women. In the unlikely medium of tapestry, Shannon Bool depicts a gleaming, unobtainable figure which reflects the Surrealists' fascination with the 'Noble Mannequin... perfect, so perfect that in her peregrinations she doesn't always bother to take her head, arms and legs with her.'[4] Using another 'feminine' medium, Kiki Smith stitches a more abject torso, like a tailor's dummy, with the site of her decapitation and her sex plastered with glass beads. This *Siren* (1994) has had her dangerous song muted, and is (as Louise Bourgeois remarked of her own sculpture) 'armless and therefore harmless'. Caitlin Keogh's sharp, graphic style descends from Surrealism via advertising and illustration, both worlds where Surrealist imagery quickly took root. She has given the blank, amputated form of the mannequin a very literal interior life by adding coiled intestines, which provide a formal echo to the draped chains and rope that hint at bondage as well as adornment.

One objective of Surrealism was to expose unflinchingly the darkest secrets of desire, in which the woman is the object or site of male fantasy. The French Surrealist writer and ethnographer Michel Leiris, contemplating an image of a hooded nude, imagined the 'satanic joy' of access to a woman's body without its troublesome head: 'her head – the sign of her individuality and intelligence – is mocked and denied. Faced with her, the partner is no longer in the presence of a "creature of God" whose face, hoist to the top of her shoulders, seems made to contemplate the stars or any other symbol of elevation and purity, but is in a position to use – with what sacrilegious power! – a simple and universal erotic mechanism.'[5] According to this reading, to make a body headless is to take away the site of the rational, thinking, individual person and to reduce it to a symbol of the female. But consider an alternative: that the beheading can be seen less as a mutilation than as a device that allows the body's experience to stand as a universal as much as a personal, autobiographical testimony. *Do Not Abandon Me* (2009–10), the collaboration between Tracey Emin and Louise Bourgeois, began as a series of headless torsos (male and female), painted by the older artist in delicate gouache wash and passed on to Emin, somewhat in the spirit of the Surrealists' game of '*cadavre exquis*' (exquisite corpse). Emin added small, spidery figures, entreaties and other fragments of narrative. Both artists are known for deeply personal and sometimes painfully honest work, but its power lies in its ability to speak to the universal.

Without a head or face, a body is anonymised, its individuality removed. By the same token, the body is freed from the controlling, rational, speaking head and released into the realm of feeling, sensation, reaction, mood or desire. Jo Ann Callis has spoken of her debt to Bellmer (particularly to the sado-masochistic depictions of his lovers Unica Zurn and Nora Mitrani), and such is evident in her images of flesh under constraint or bearing the marks of bondage. Even when her photographs are not explicit or even obviously about sex, they seem to deal with very specific desires. By focusing on these private moments, enactments of the fantasies of the female protagonist, Callis absolves us of the lurking sense of voyeurism that Bellmer's work can arouse.

Penny Slinger, a fixture of swinging London in the late 1960s and early '70s, was directly linked to the Surrealists thorough the patronage of Roland Penrose, who had bought the work from her degree show. The collages that make up her cycle *An Exorcism* (1970–77) use photographs she took a few years before in a derelict gothic mansion, some brutal in their treatment of her own image. For the artist, however, the action of collage was a putting-together of the pieces of her life, a journey of recovery from a psychic disintegration. 'In the process of sorting and distilling the archetypes, I felt myself emerging from the nightmare of others' projections', she later wrote.

---

1. Merriam Webster Dictionary reported 'surreal' as its trending word of the year in December 2016.
2. Eileen Agar, *A Look at My Life*, Methuen, London, 1988.
3. Mary Ann Caws, *Seeing the Surrealist Woman: We Are a Problem, Surrealism and Women*, MIT Press, Cambridge, Massachussets, 1991.
4. René Crevel, *Minotaure*, no.5, February 1934.
5. Michel Leiris, 'The Caput Mortuum or the Alchemists Wife', *Documents*, no.8, 1930.

Shannon Bool

Shannon Bool was born in 1972 in Comox, Canada, and lives and works in Berlin. She attended the Emily Carr Institute of Art and Design, Vancouver; The Cooper Union, New York; and the Städelschule, Frankfurt am Main. In 2013 Bool was artist in residence at the Villa Romana, Florence. Solo exhibitions include CRAC Alsace (2010); Bonner Kunstverein, Bonn (2011); Contemporary Art Gallery, Vancouver (2015); and Illingworth Kerr Gallery, Calgary (2016). Group shows include La Biennale de Montréal (2016); 'Boom She Boom', Museum für Moderne Kunst, Frankfurt am Main (2015); Klöntal Trienale, Kunsthaus Glarus (2014); 'Soft Pictures', Fondazione Sandretto Re Rebaudengo, Turin (2013); and 'Made in Germany', Sprengel Museum, Hanover (2012).

21

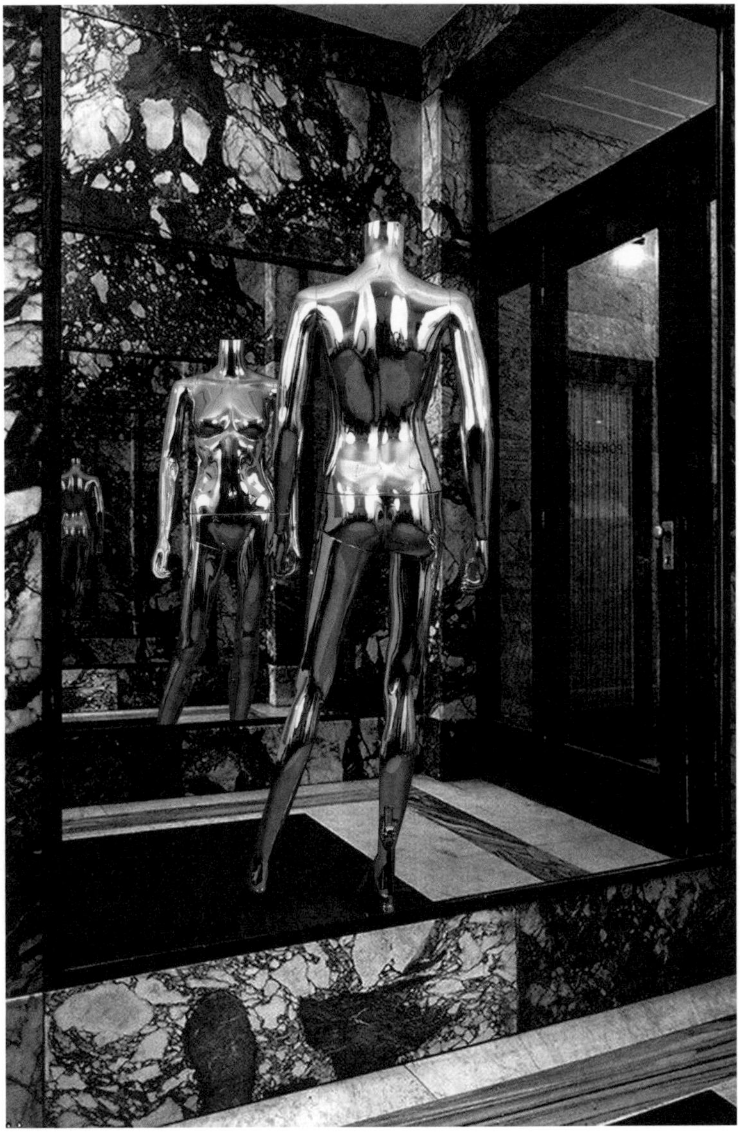

Michaelerplatz 3
2016
Wool tapestry
289.6 x 188 cm

Kiki Smith

Kiki Smith was born in 1954 in Nuremberg, Germany and lives and works in New York. She is recognised for her multidisciplinary practice, incorporating sculpture, glassmaking, printmaking, watercolour, photography and textiles, among other production methods, through which she explores the body, mortality, regeneration, gender politics and the interconnection of spirituality and the natural world. A major retrospective opened at the San Francisco Museum of Art (2005), touring to Walker Art Center, Minneapolis, Contemporary Arts Museum, Houston, Whitney Museum of American Art, New York and La Coleccion Jumex, Mexico City. In 2016 Smith was awarded the International Sculpture Center's Lifetime Achievement in Contemporary Sculpture Award.

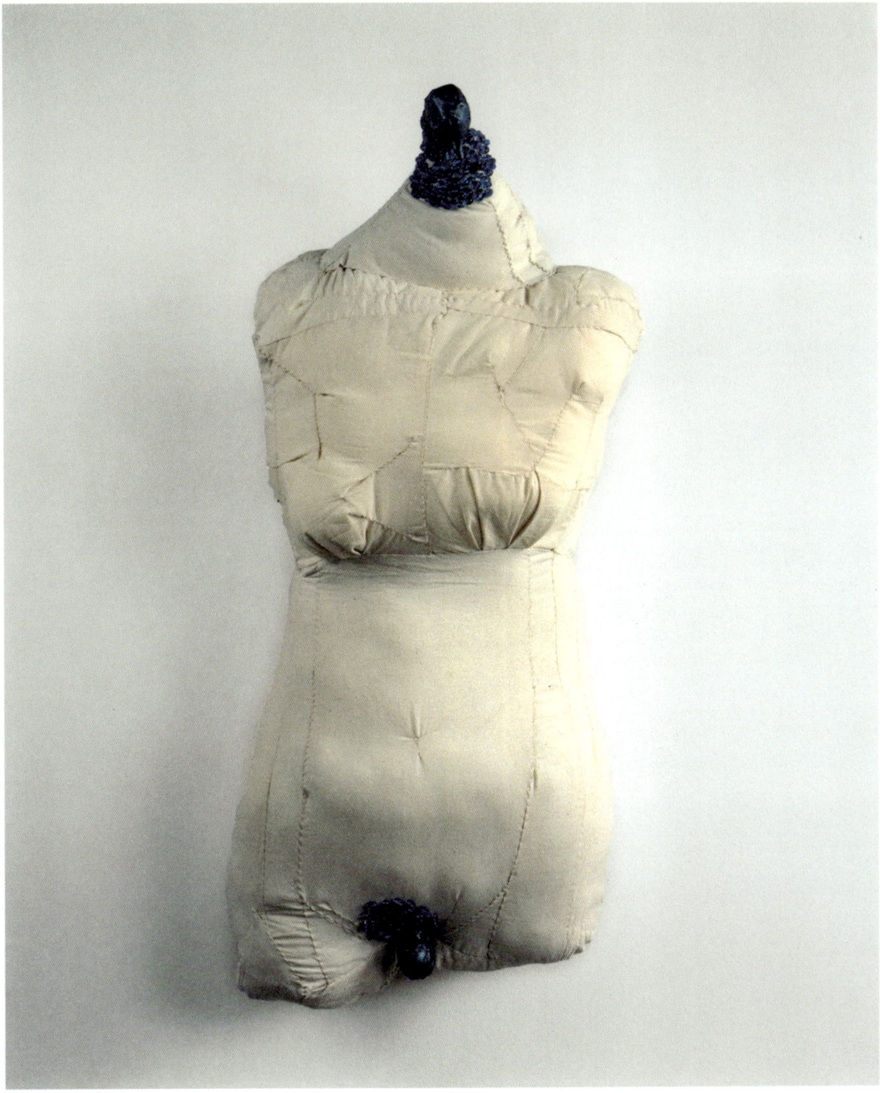

Siren
1994
Muslin, fibrefill, anodised aluminium and glass beads
94 x 38.1 x 38.1 cm

Caitlin Keogh

Caitlin Keogh was born in 1982 in Alaska and lives and works in Brooklyn, New York. She received her MFA from the Milton Avery Graduate School of the Arts, Bard, in 2011. Her first museum solo exhibition, 'Good Value, Fine Quality', was held at MoMA PS1, New York (2012). Recent group exhibitions include 'The Hole', Künstlerhaus Bremen, Germany; 'Flatlands', Whitney Museum of American Art, New York (both 2016); and 'Sinister Feminism',12th A.I.R. Gallery Biennial, Brooklyn (2017).

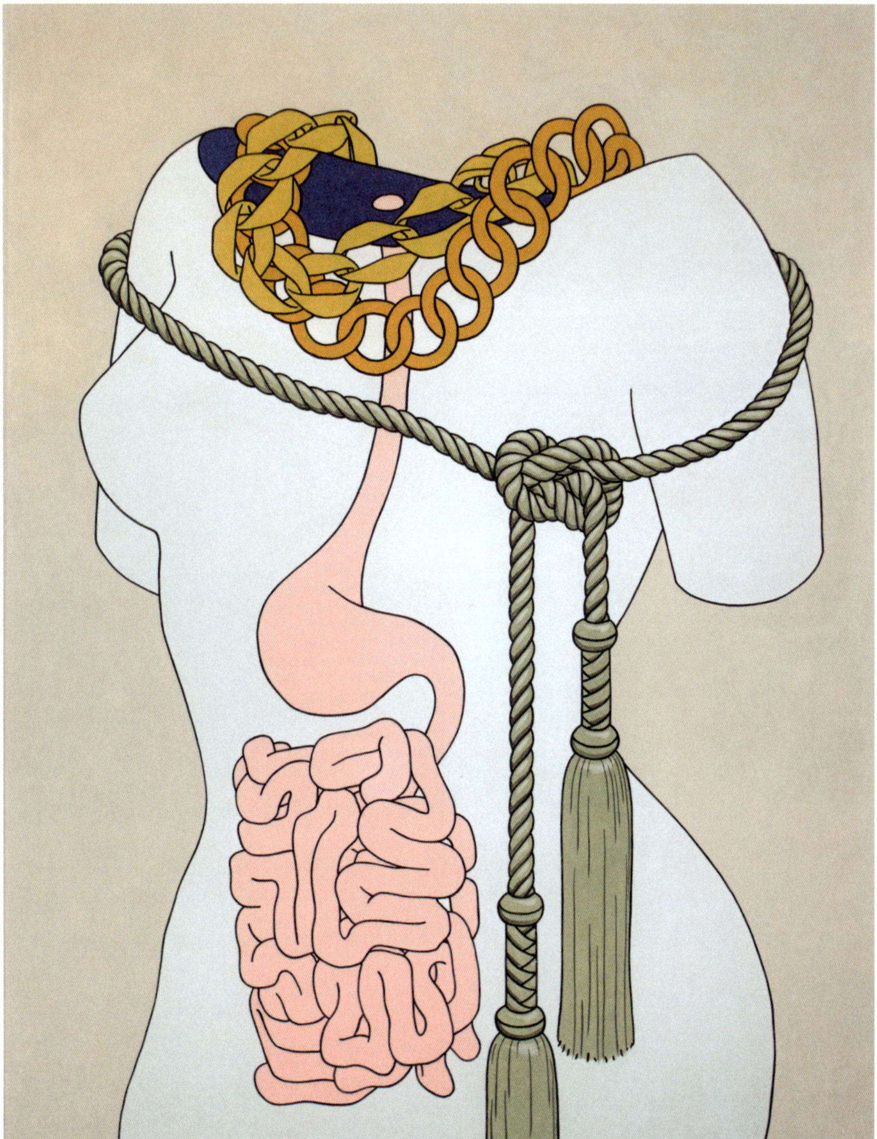

Intestine and Tassels
2015
Acrylic on canvas
213.6 x 160 cm

Louise Bourgeois
& Tracey Emin

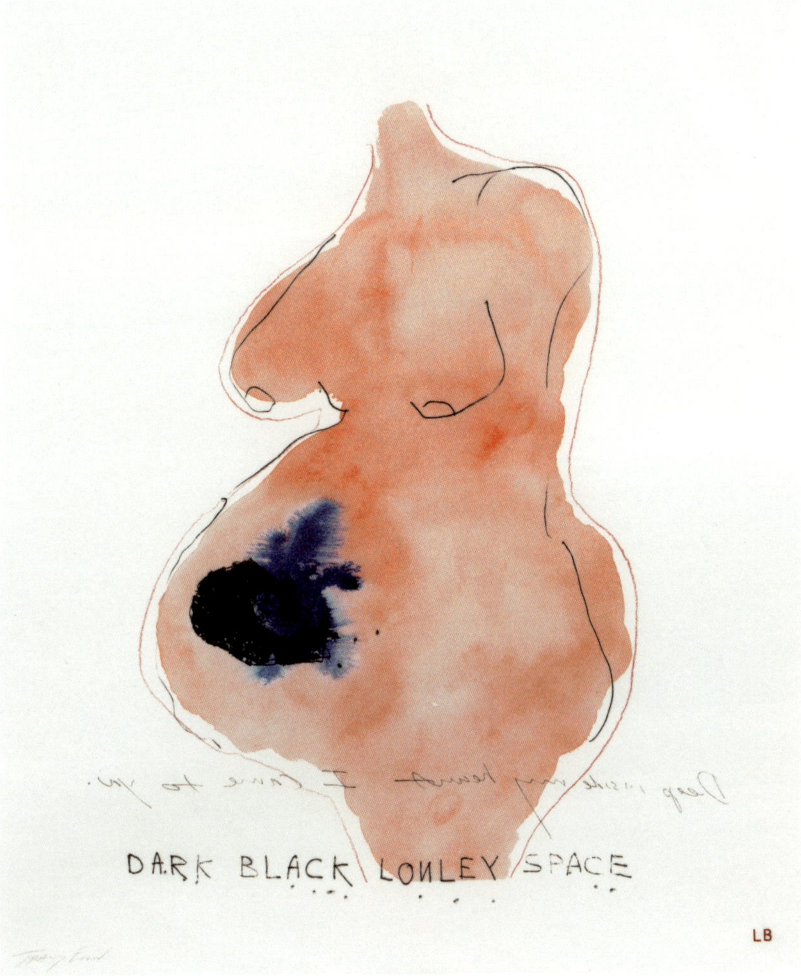

Deep inside my heart
2009–10
Archival dyes printed on cloth
76.2 x 61 cm

Jo Ann Callis

Jo Ann Callis was born in 1940 in Cincinnati and relocated to Los Angeles in 1961. She enrolled at the University of California, Los Angeles in 1970 where she began taking classes with Robert Heinecken. She started teaching at CalArts in 1976 and remains a faculty member of the Photography and Media programme. Her work has been exhibited in such venues as the Museum of Modern Art, New York; Los Angeles County Museum of Art; Hammer Museum, Los Angeles; Museum of Contemporary Art, Los Angeles; and San Francisco Museum of Modern Art. A retrospective of her work, 'Woman Twirling', was held at the J Paul Getty Museum, Los Angeles (2009). Callis has received three National Endowment for the Arts Fellowships and a Guggenheim Fellowship.

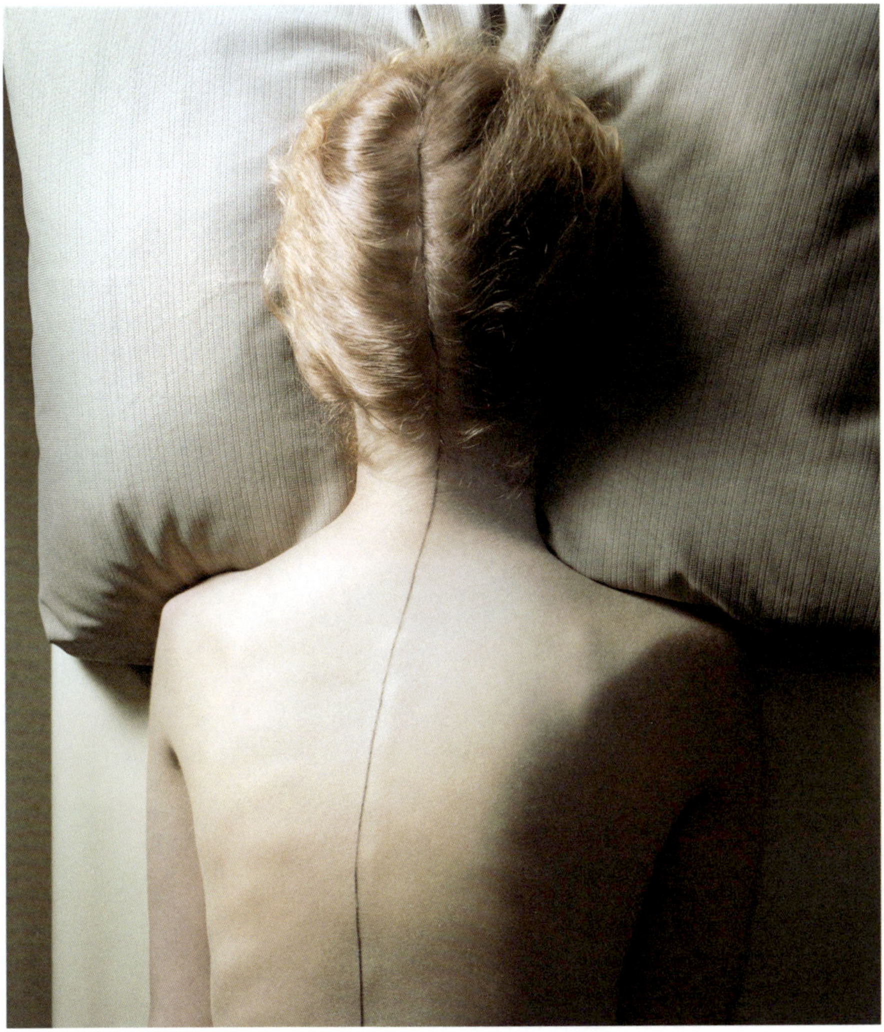

Untitled (Woman with Black Line)
c.1976
Archival pigment print, from *Early Color Portfolio*
40.6 x 50.8 cm

Penny Slinger

Penny Slinger was born in 1947 in London. She studied at Chelsea College of Arts, London, left Britain for the Caribbean in 1979 and now lives and works in California. She first exhibited in 'Young and Fantastic', Institute of Contemporary Arts, London (1969) and won critical attention for provocative works that explore feminine power through the appropriation of the visual language of Surrealism. Recent group exhibitions have been held at Manchester Art Gallery; Tate St Ives, UK (both 2009); Trondheim Kunstmuseum (2013); BOZAR – Centre for Fine Arts, Brussels (2014); Hamburger Kunsthalle, Hamburg; and Hayward Gallery, London (both 2015).

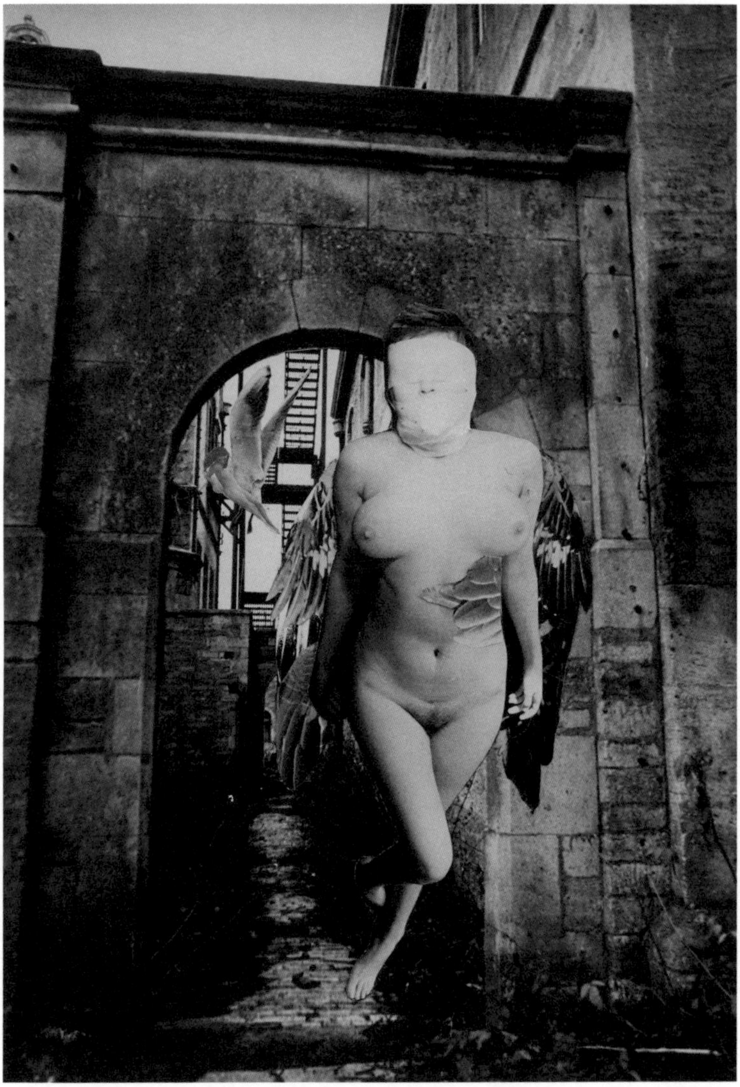

Flying Blind (The Feminine Mystique)
1977
Photo-collage
48.5 x 33 cm

‘I warn you, I refuse to be an object.’[6]

The ideal surrealist object is something plucked from its normal place in the world and made to seem strange and new, exploiting the capacity of objects to unsettle us by embodying our deepest desires and fears. Mona Hatoum's *Jardin Public* (1993), with its punning, witty title in the tradition of the readymade, is a perfect surrealist object; a metal garden chair arrestingly sexualised by the addition of a triangle of pubic hair to the seat. While playful, the elision of woman and object carries a disturbing charge. There is a bawdy comedy in the phallic cast vegetables of Helen Chadwick's *I Thee Wed* (1993), each thrust through a furry ring. Nevine Mahmoud's *Miss her (peach)* (2017) plays on the age-old association of fruit, flower and female sexuality, something that DH Lawrence makes most lasciviously explicit: 'showing her crimson through the purple slit / Like a wound, the exposure of her secret, on the open day. / Like a prostitute, the bursten fig, making a show of her secret.'[7] Rendered in cool, smooth marble and alabaster (a masculine medium mastered), it is inviting but idealised, like the flesh of classical statuary. Chairs are again pressed to stand in for bodies in *The Kiss* (2003), by Sarah Lucas, in which one chair, designated female by target-like breasts made in cigarettes, sits in the lap of another chair, impaled on its equally cartoonish cigarette-outlined penis. Like Emin and Bourgeois, Lucas turns a female gaze on a sometimes vulnerable or absurd male body. Rather than making an object stand for the body, Alina Szapocznikow removes her own body – in the form of casts of lips, breast or hand – to the status of a fetishised object in the world. Julia Phillips' impressions of her body are fashioned into ceramic devices suggesting purposes of restraint, ritual or fetish, while the fragility of the material locates them somewhere between ornament and implement.

Objectification is the charge against misogynists: in the feminist lexicon the fetish denotes the exploitative, fragmenting male gaze of advertising, pornography and art. Making parts of the female body into literal objects is a way to own and ironise this gaze. The body as still life operates in the sphere of the domestic and in a genre traditionally assigned to women, meanwhile infusing it with a challenge. In Edith Rimmington's 1951 work *Museum*, a female bust is displayed under glass, and while her own eyes are shut, the scrutiny of many is returned and rebuked by the staring eyes multiplying across her face. Offered up for a different kind of attention, Linder's iconic 1977 image updates surrealist collage with punk attitude, merging two available archetypes of womanhood by giving a porn model's gleaming torso an electric iron as a head. Laurie Simmons makes similarly ironic commentary on consumerism and feminism in her dreamlike scenarios of *Walking Objects*, domestic items anthropomorphised with shapely legs. Lee Miller, surely the most objectified woman of Surrealism, owner of the torso, breast and neck obsessively photographed by Man Ray, is also the author of the startling image *Untitled (Severed breast from radical surgery in a place setting 2)* (c.1929), the object of desire served up as a grisly meal on a humble place setting. A high kitsch version of surreality provides the perfect expression of contemporary anxieties in the videos of Shana Moulton, whose alter-ego, Cynthia, is overwhelmed by the products, prescriptions drugs and New-Age spriritualism on offer in her sugary, psychedelic world.

The surreal object is closely related to Freud's idea of the fetish: a stand-in on which desire is focused and displaced. As Leiris again wrote: 'the source of erotic fetishism [...] is very close to religious fetishism and the cult of relics because it manifests the same type of magical thought in that the part is taken for the whole, the accessory for the person, and that the part is not just equal to the whole, but is even stronger for it.'[8] Hair is the most eroticised and lasting of bodily materials. While attached to the head it symbolises femininity and incites lust: out of place or separated from the body, it provokes repulsion. Surviving beyond the body as a relic, it functions as a symbol of loss and therefore memory, a potent charge that Hatoum has harnessed on other occasions. A K Dolven makes a head of hair unfamiliar with a simple inversion, so that blonde tresses become softly waving fronds, or an eyeless creature ambiguously cradled or controlled in male hands. In a disquieting blurring of bodily boundaries, the young French painter Julie Curtiss depicts a Venus entirely made up of coiled tresses. Both seductive and repulsive, this signifier of femininity is in excess and takes on the quality of viscera, indecently exposed.

6. Leonora Carrington, fundacionleonoracarrington.org
7. DH Lawrence, *Birds, Beasts and Flowers: Poems*, Martin Secker, London, 1923.
8. Leiris, *ibid*.

Mona Hatoum

Mona Hatoum was born in 1952 into a Palestinian family in Beirut, Lebanon, and lives and works in London and Berlin. Recent museum solo exhibitions include Pinacoteca do Estado, São Paulo (2014); Centre Pompidou, Paris (2015); and Tate Modern, London (2016). She has participated in numerous important group exhibitions including The Turner Prize (1995); the Venice Biennale (1995 and 2005); Documenta 11, Kassel (2002); Biennale of Sydney (2006); the Istanbul Biennial (1995 and 2011); and the Fifth Moscow Biennale of Contemporary Art (2013). In 2016 she was awarded the SMFA Medal by the School of the Museum of Fine Arts, Boston.

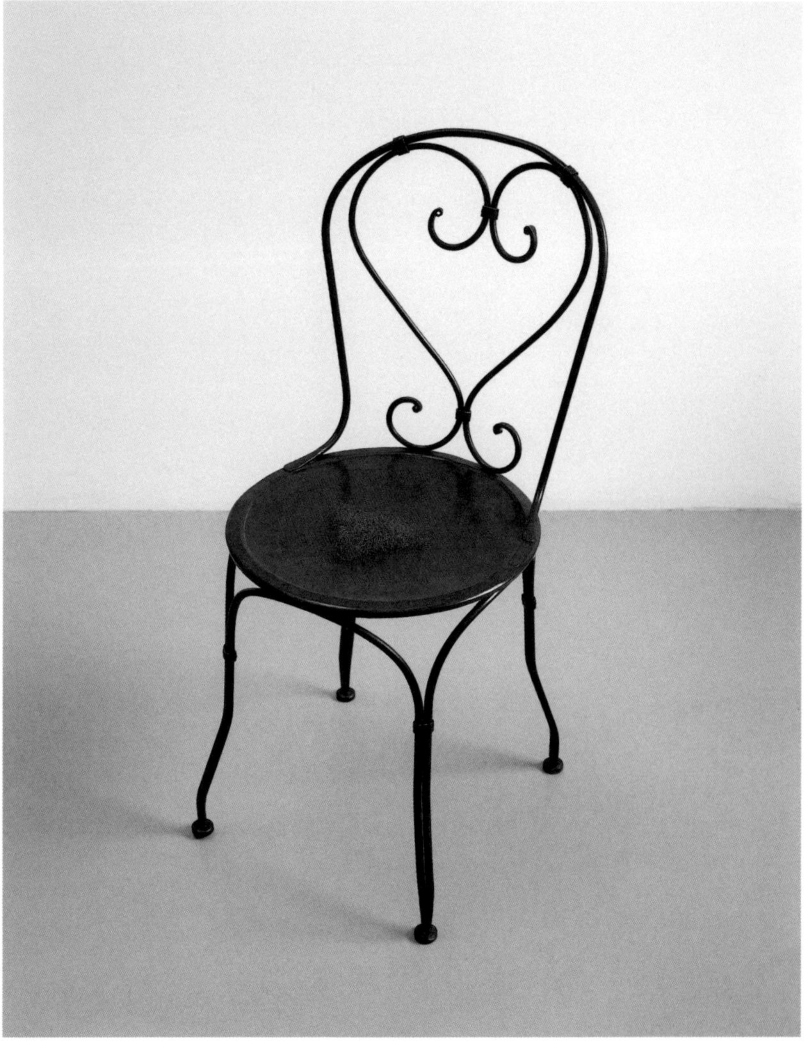

Jardin Public
1993
Painted wrought iron, wax and pubic hair
88.5 x 39.5 x 49 cm

Helen Chadwick

Helen Chadwick (1953–96) was born in Croydon, UK, and studied at Brighton Polytechnic and Chelsea College of Art, London, where she went on to teach. She was nominated for the Turner Prize in 1987. Chadwick had a number of significant solo exhibitions in her lifetime, including 'Of Mutability', Institute of Contemporary Arts, London (1986); 'Effluvia', Serpentine Gallery, London (1994); and 'Bad Blooms', Museum of Modern Art, New York (1995). In 2004, a major retrospective of Chadwick's work opened at the Barbican Art Gallery, London.

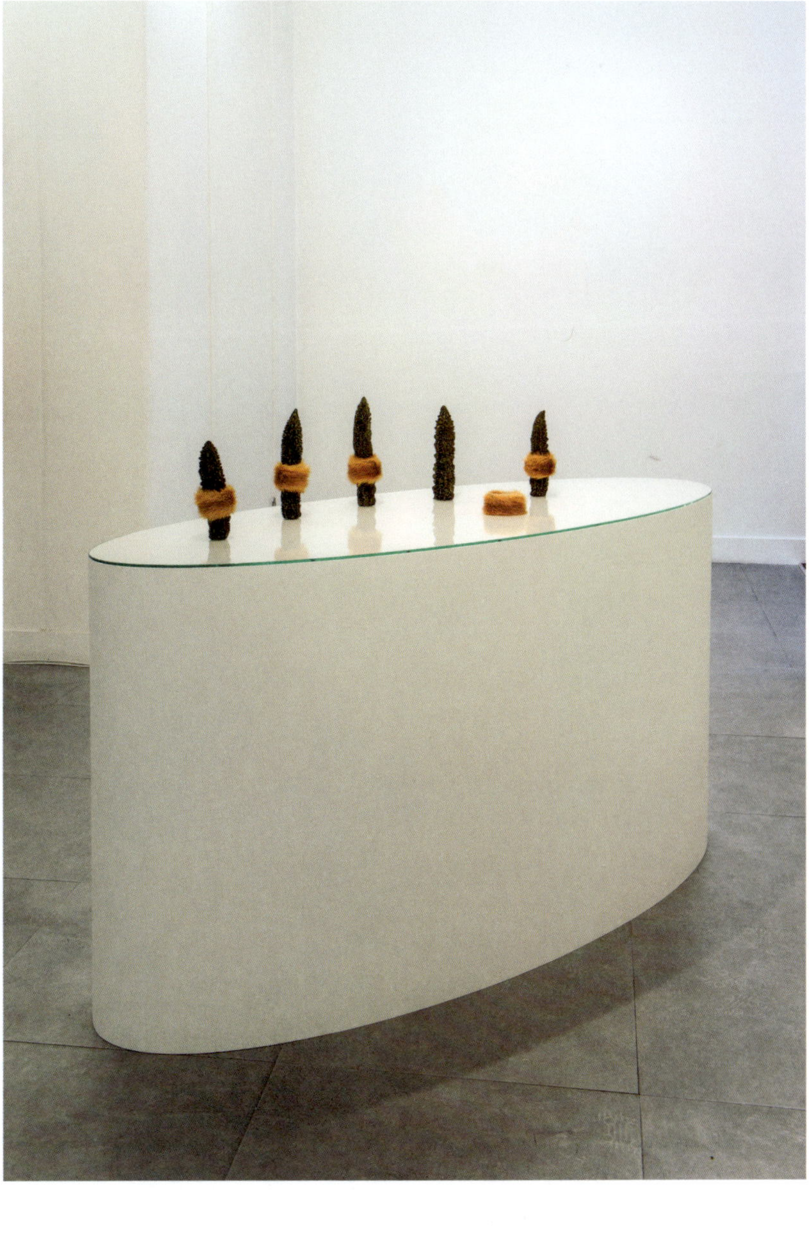

I Thee Wed
1993
Set of 5 cast bronze vegetables, fur, glass and painted plywood
Overall dimensions: 85 x 152 x 60 cm

Nevine Mahmoud

Nevine Mahmoud was born in 1988 in London and lives and works in Los Angeles. She received her BA from Goldsmiths, University of London and her MFA from the University of Southern California, Los Angeles. She has participated in numerous group exhibitions, including most recently 'The Poet, the Critic and the Missing', Museum of Contemporary Art, Los Angeles; 'The Lasting Concept', Portland Institute of Contemporary Art; and 'This Is Presence', Ballroom Marfa, Texas (all 2016).

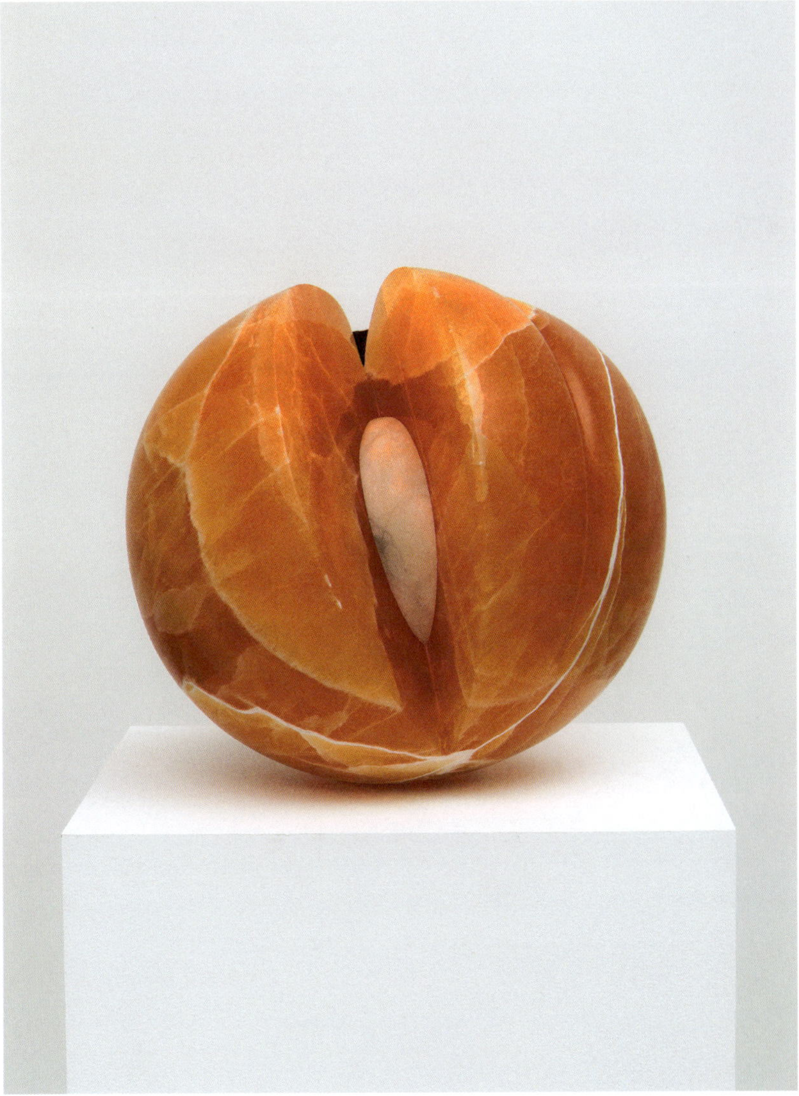

Miss her (peach)
2017
Calcite, marble and steel
30.5 x 25.4 x 25.4 cm

Sarah Lucas

Sarah Lucas was born in 1962 in London and lives and works in Suffolk, UK. After leaving school at 16, she studied at the Working Men's College, London College of Printmaking and the Goldsmiths College. In 1988, her work was included in the group exhibition, 'Freeze' and she became known as one of the leading figures in the generation of Young British Artists that emerged in the 1990s. Recent solo exhibitions include 'NOB + Gelatin', Secession, Vienna (2013); 'POWER IN WOMAN', Sir John Soane's Museum, London (2016); and 'Good Muse', Legion of Honour, San Francisco (2017). Recent group exhibitions include 'Self-Portrait', Louisiana Museum of Modern Art, Humlebaek (2012); 'Performing for the Camera', Tate Modern, London (2016); and 'No Place Like Home', Israel Museum, Jerusalem (2017). Lucas represented Britain at the 56th Venice Biennale (2015).

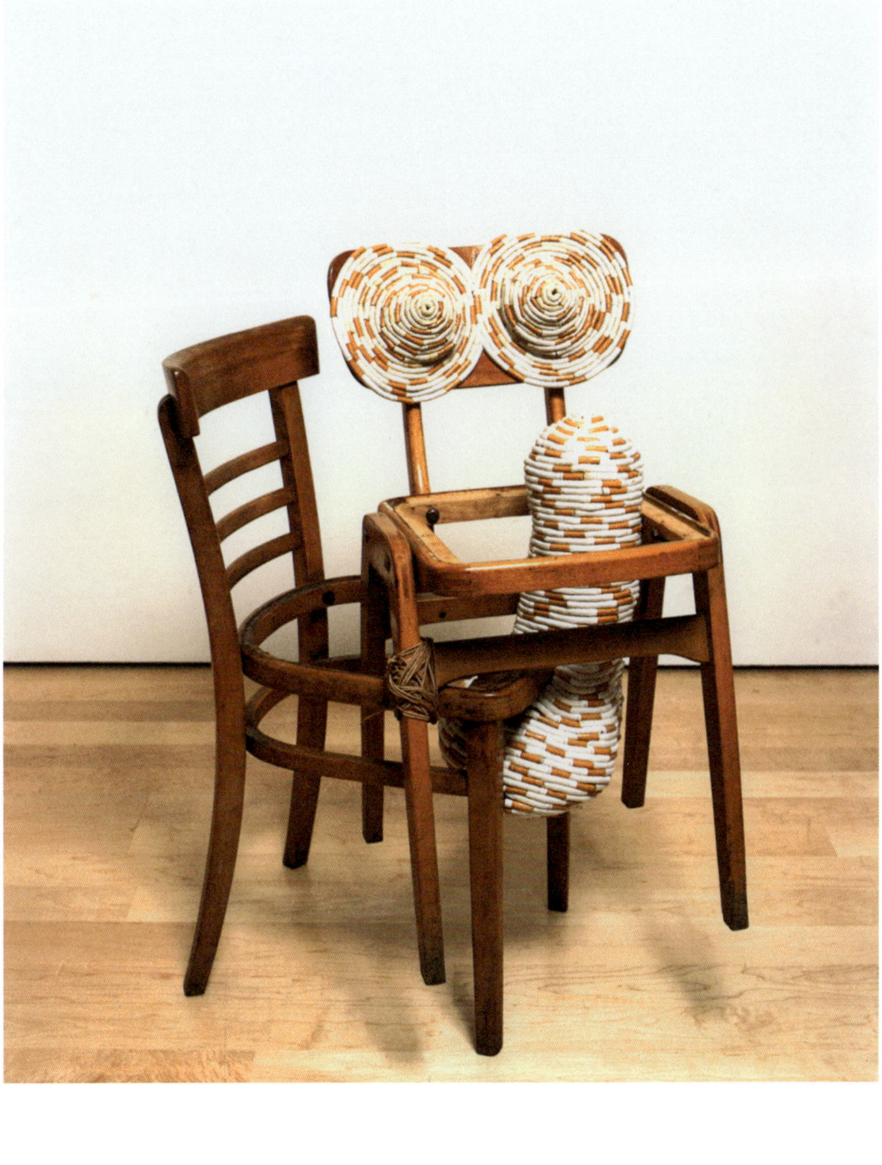

The Kiss
2003
Cigarettes, two chairs, leather cord, varnish and glue
90.5 x 63 x 70 cm

Alina Szapocznikow

Alina Szapocznikow (1926–73) was born in Kalisz, Poland. After surviving the concentration camps during World War II, she moved to Prague where she studied sculpture in the studio of Otto Wagner, among others, and then in Paris at the École des Beaux-Arts. Having returned to Poland in 1951, Szapocznikow represented Poland in the 31st Venice Biennale (1962), thereafter moving back to Paris at a historically vital time, when artists from Marcel Duchamp to Yves Klein were simultaneously developing work in response to Formalism. In recent years, Szapocznikow has been the subject of numerous major international exhibitions, including the first comprehensive retrospective that opened at WIELS Contemporary Art Centre, Brussels (2011), touring to New York, Los Angeles and Columbus; as well as a major survey at the Centre Pompidou, Paris (2013).

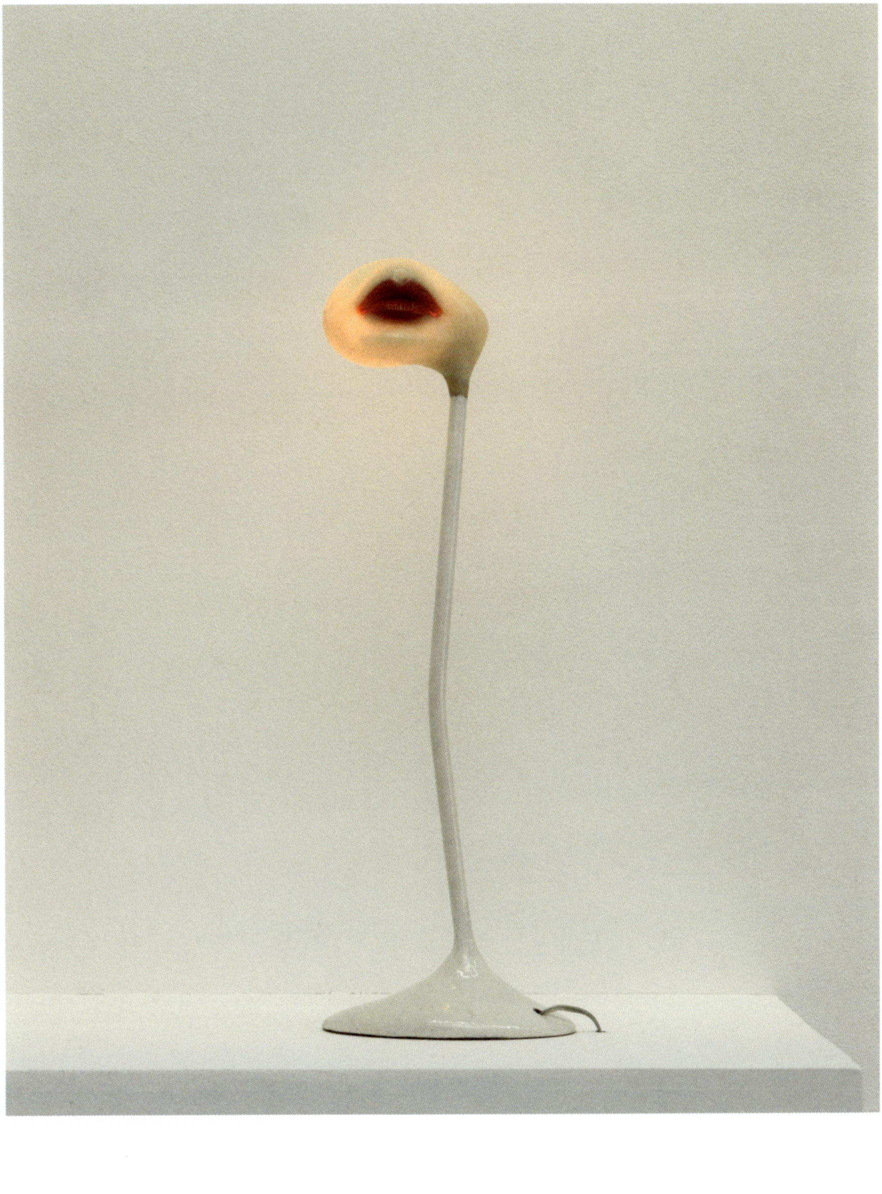

Lampe-Bouche
1966
Coloured polyester resin, electrical wiring and metal
48 x 16 x 13 cm

Julia Phillips

Julia Phillips was born in 1985 in Hamburg and lives and works in New York. She received her MFA from Columbia University School of the Arts, New York (2015) and participated in the Whitney Museum's Independent Study Program (2015). She has had solo exhibitions at Hochschule für bildende Künste Hamburg (2012); Hinterconti, Hamburg (2013); and Campoli Presi, London (2016). Group exhibitions include 'Index 12', Kunsthaus Hamburg (2012) and 'The Feminist Sex Shoppe', On The Ground Floor, Los Angeles (2015).

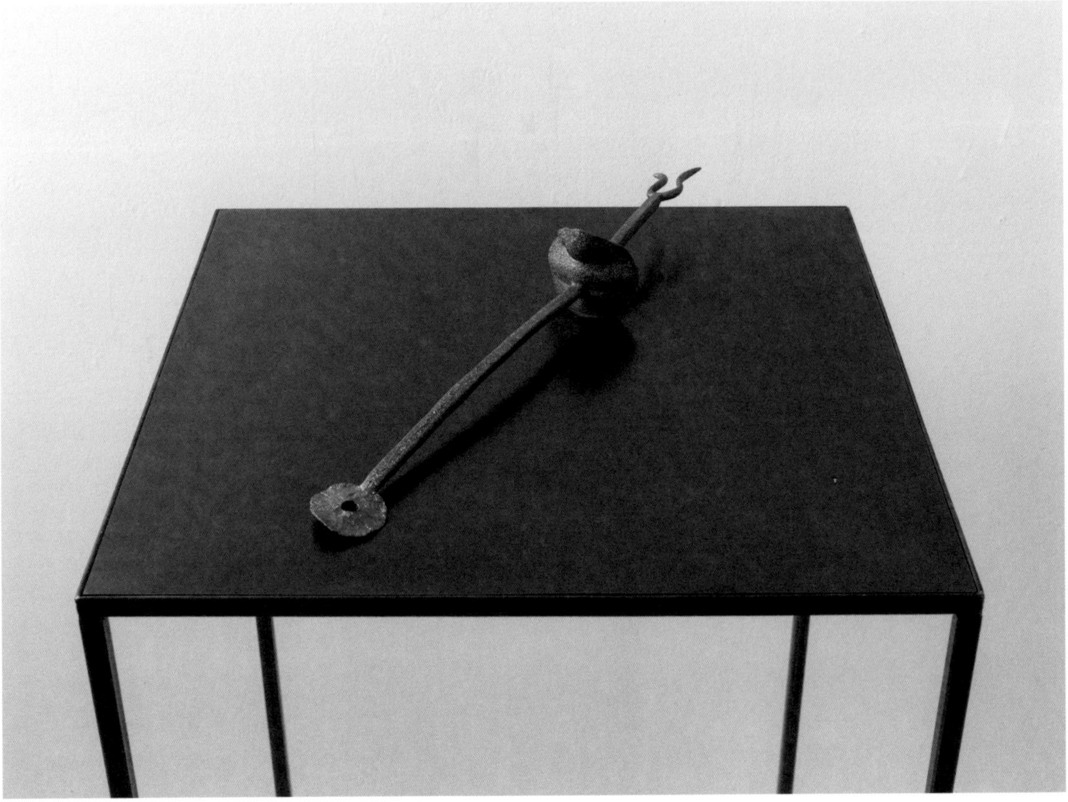

Penetrator (#2)
2016
Salt glazed, wood fired ceramics and metal pedestal
100.3 x 39.4 x 39.4 cm

Edith Rimmington

Edith Rimmington (1902–86) was born in Leicester, UK, and studied at the Brighton School of Art. In London in 1937 she was introduced to the British Surrealist Group and became one of its few female members. As well as producing paintings and photography, Rimmington wrote poetry, often through the practice of automatic writing, and contributed to Surrealist publications. Most recently, her work has featured in group exhibitions including 'Angels of Anarchy', Manchester Art Gallery (2009); 'The Colour of My Dreams', Vancouver Art Gallery (2011); and 'The Mythic Method: Classicism in British Art 1920–1950', Pallant House Gallery, Chichester, UK (2016).

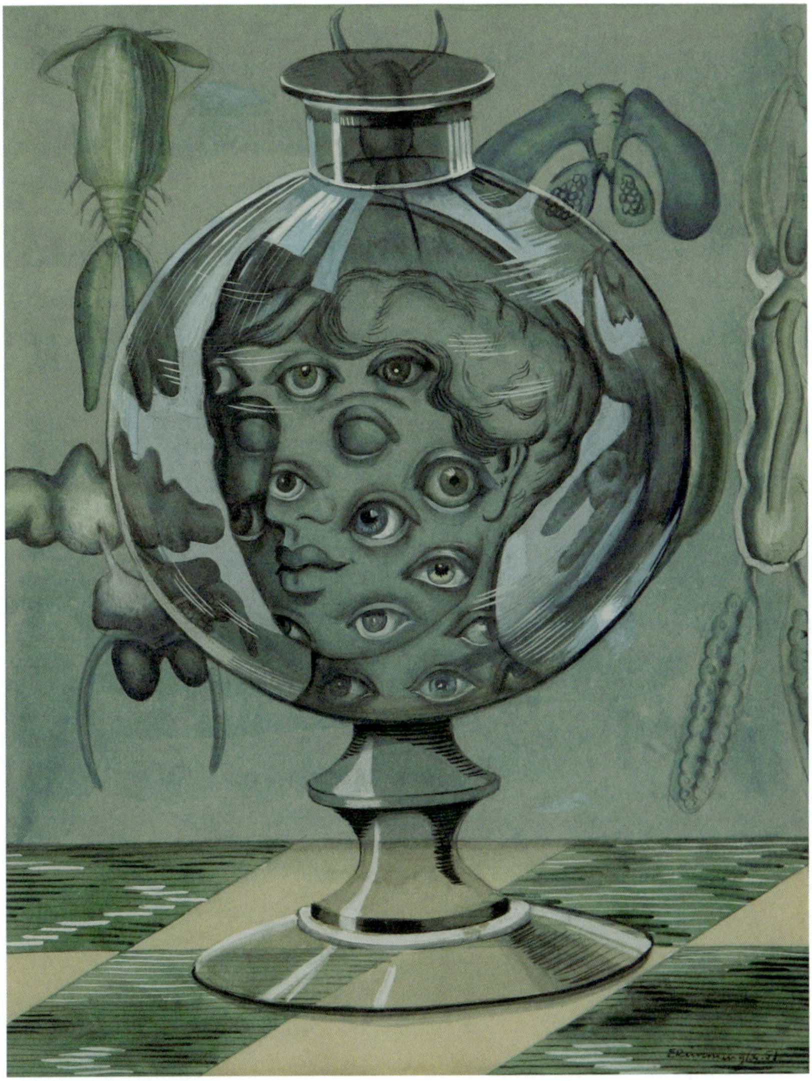

Museum
1951
Gouache on paper
32 x 23.5 cm

Linder

Linder was born Linda Mulvey in 1954 in Liverpool and lives and works in Heysham, UK. She became Linder in Manchester in the 1970s, embracing punk's transformative energy, and created posters and album covers for her punk contemporaries, including, most famously, the Buzzcocks' *Orgasm Addict* in 1977. Selected solo exhibitions include Chisenhale Gallery, London (2010); Tate St Ives, UK; and Musée d'Art moderne de la Ville de Paris (both 2013). Recent group exhibitions include 'Post Pop: East Meets West', Saatchi Gallery, London (2014); 'Nude: art from the Tate Collection', Art Gallery of New South Wales, Sydney (2016); and 'As Above, So Below', Irish Museum of Modern Art, Dublin (2017).

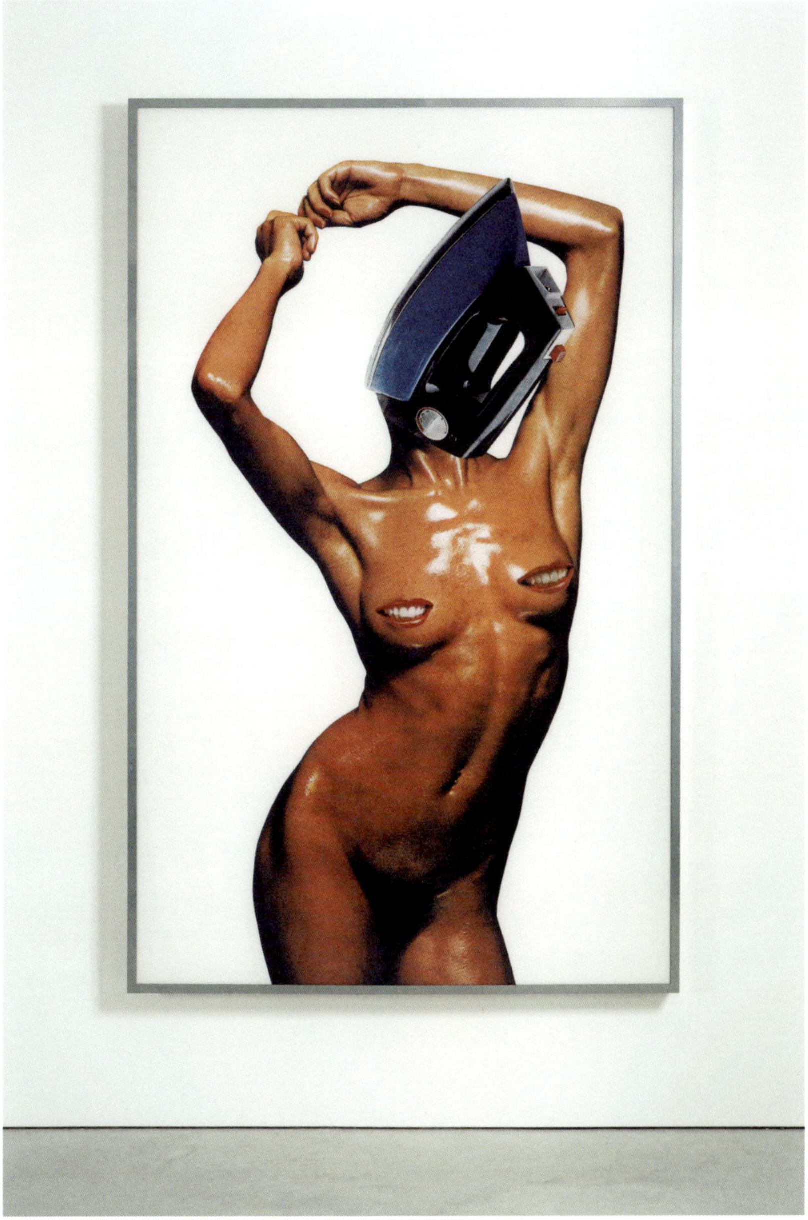

It's The Buzz, Cock!
2015
Duratrans on light box
251 x 153 x 10 cm

Laurie Simmons

Laurie Simmons was born in 1949 in Long Island, New York, and lives and works in New York. She studied at the Tyler School of Art, Philadelphia, and started, in her early work, staging fictional scenes, using dolls and miniature objects. Simmons has been the subject of significant museum retrospectives, including San Jose Museum of Art, California (1990); Baltimore Museum of Art, Maryland (1997); and Gothenburg Museum of Art, Sweden (2012). Recent group exhibitions include 'This Will Have Been', Museum of Contemporary Art, Chicago (2012); 'All You Need Is Love', Mori Art Museum, Tokyo (2013); and 'America Is Hard to See', Whitney Museum of American Art, New York (2015).

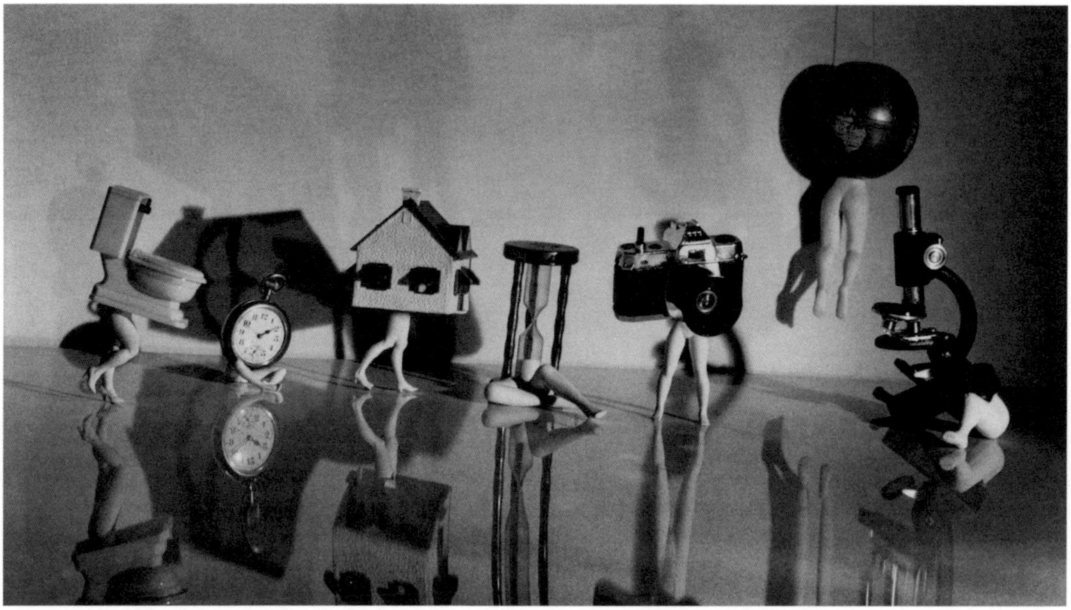

Magnum Opus II (the Bye-Bye)
1991
Gelatin silver print
137.2 x 241.3 cm

Lee Miller

Lee Miller (1907–77) was born in Poughkeepsie, New York, and moved to Paris in 1929, where she worked with Surrealist artist and photographer Man Ray before establishing her own studio. She became known as a portraitist and fashion photographer, but her most enduring body of work is that of her Surrealist images. In 1944, Miller worked as a correspondent for the US army across Europe and became one of very few female photo-journalists to cover the front-line. She has been the subject of a number of retrospectives, including 'The Art of Lee Miller', Victoria and Albert Museum, London (2008), touring to Jeu de Paume, Paris and San Francisco Museum of Modern Art; and 'Lee Miller: Surrealist Photographer', Museo de Arte Moderno, Mexico City (2015).

53

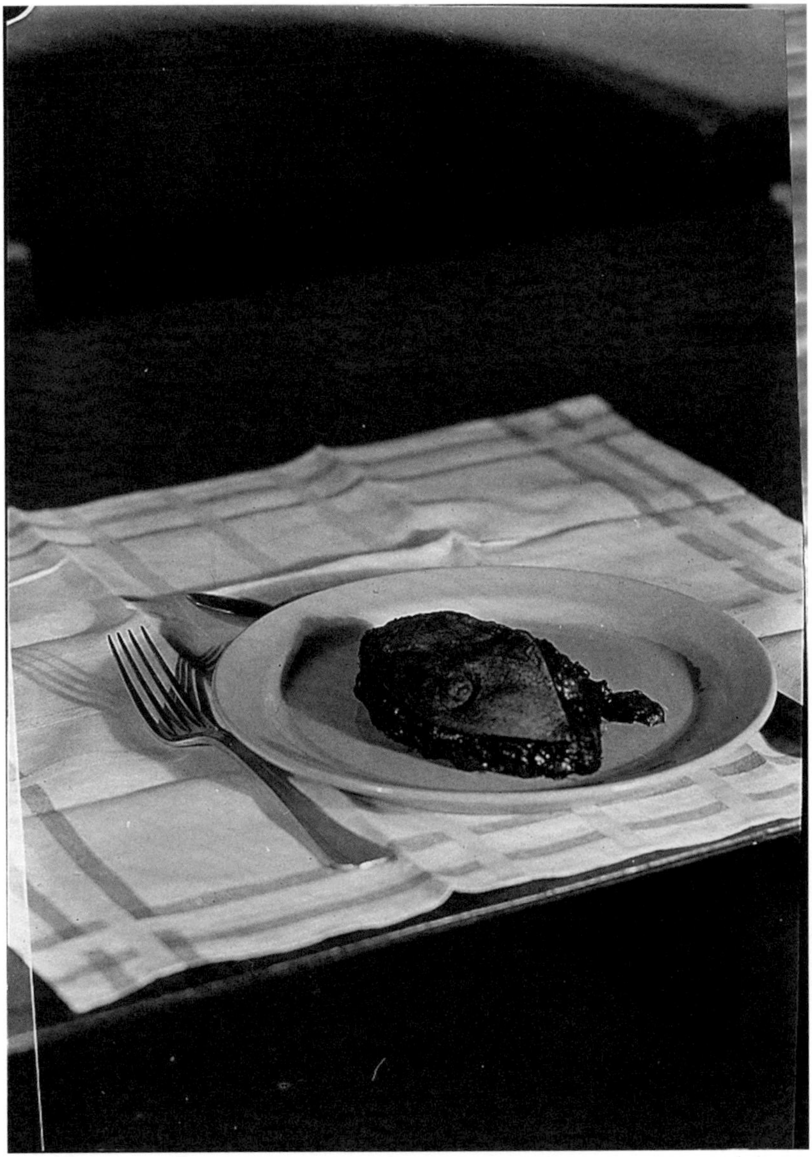

Untitled [Severed breast from radical surgery in a place setting 2],
Paris, France c.1929
Vintage print
15.4 x 10.5 cm

Shana Moulton

Shana Moulton was born in 1976 in Oakhurst, California, and lives and works in Los Angeles. She attended the University of California, Berkeley; Carnegie Mellon University, Pittsburgh; the Skowhegan School of Painting and Sculpture; and De Ateliers, Amsterdam. Her video work has been screened and exhibited internationally, including, most recently, 'Control: Technology in Culture', Yerba Buena Center for the Arts, San Francisco (2015); 'Gund Commons', MOCA Cleveland (2016); and 'Outhouse Portal', NICC Brussels (2017). In 2016, she contributed to the group exhibitions 'Experimental People', High Line, New York; 'Bedlam', Wellcome Collection, London; and 'Your Memories Are Our Future', Palais de Tokyo and ACRUSH, Zurich.

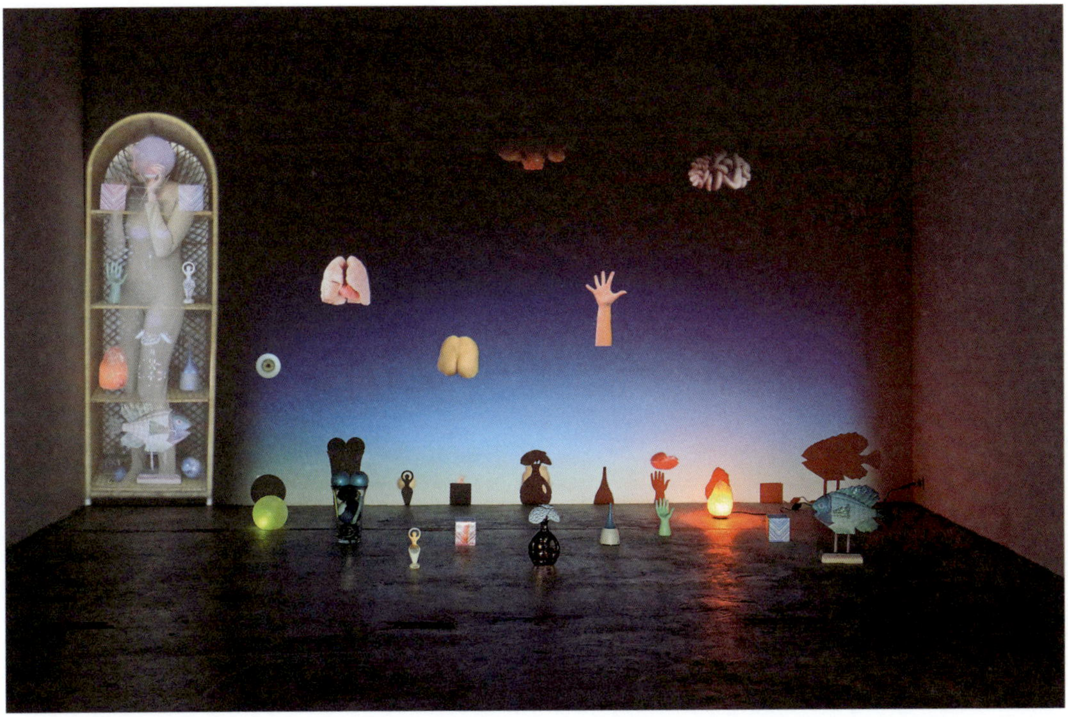

My Life as an INFJ
2015–16
HD video, lamps and objects
Dimensions variable

A K Dolven

A K Dolven was born in 1953 in Oslo and lives and works in London and Lofoten, Norway. In painting, video, installation and sound, she explores the subtle and unconscious mechanisms at play in perception, memory and emotion. Dolven has been the subject of recent solo exhibitions including 'Looking for Balance', Platform China, Beijing (2010); 'please return', Ikon Gallery, Birmingham (2015); and 'A Other Teenager', OSL contemporary, Oslo (2016).

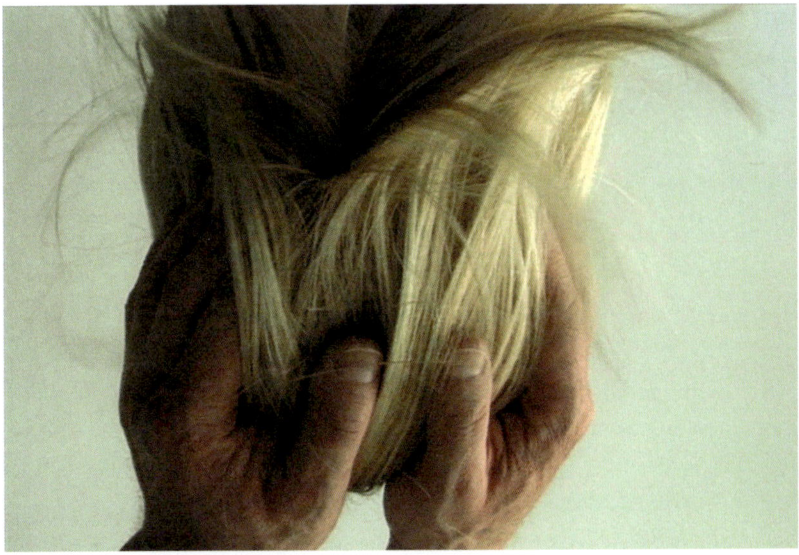

I Hold your Head in my Hands
1999
Digital video
Duration: 3 minutes 43 seconds

Julie Curtiss

Julie Curtiss was born in 1982 in France and lives and works in Brooklyn, New York. She studied at the École nationale supérieure des beaux-arts, Paris, and the School of the Art Institute in Chicago. Upon graduating, she moved to Tokyo for a year, which was a pivotal moment for her artistic development; influenced by the local art scene and Japanese graphic imagery, she started a new body of work focusing on drawing. She received a Van Lier Fellowship from the New York Foundation of the Arts in 2012.

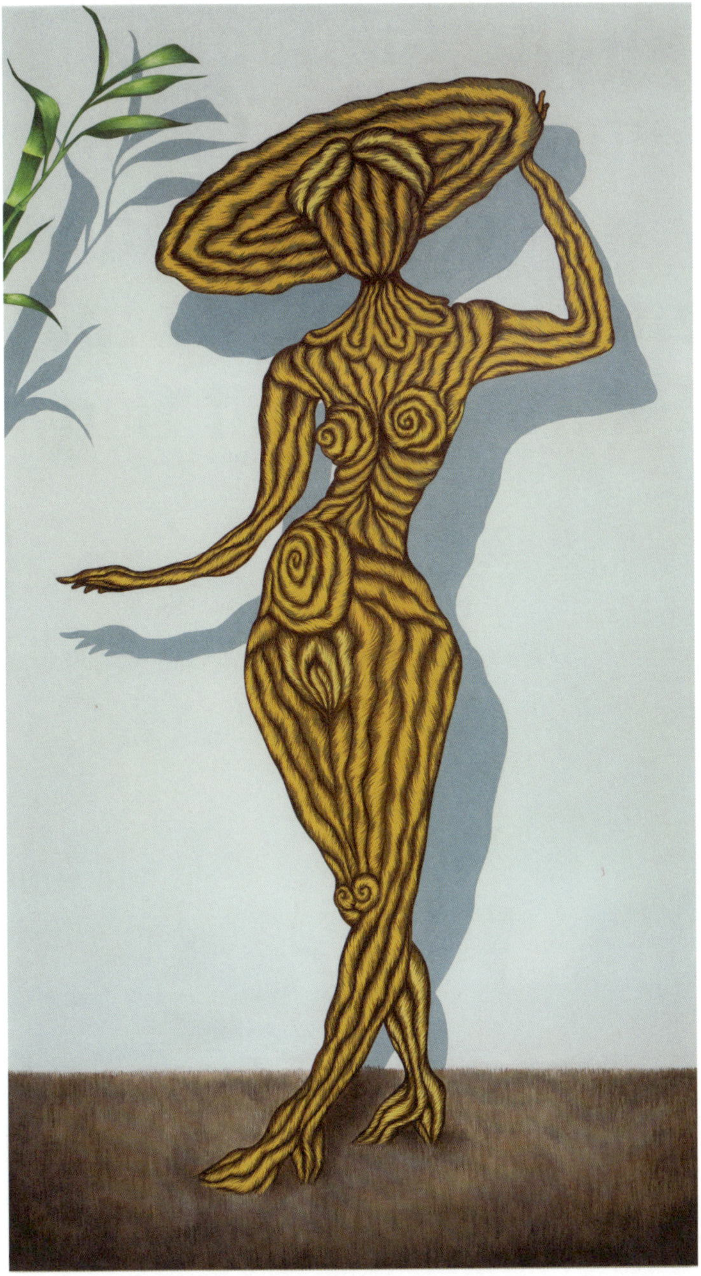

Venus
2016
Acrylic and oil on canvas
147.3 x 81.3 cm

'..of all the manifestations of the ephemeral, the human body is the most vulnerable, the only source of all joy, all suffering, all truth.'[9]

Alina Szapocznikow, whose work sits somewhere between Surrealism and the European pop of Nouveau Réalisme, achieved a radical reimaging of the body and of sculpture in her fragile 'awkward objects'. Humorous, political, eroticised, always threatening disintegration, they are her attempt to fix 'the fleeting moments of life... the traces of the body'. The body – fragmented, misshapen, missing parts – surfaces repeatedly in Rosemarie Trockel's multifarious and influential practice. Resistant to definition, but always informed by gender politics and infused with irony, her work encompasses rough-hewn ceramics as well as objects or imagery juxtaposed to startling, surrealist effect.

Tethering cast bronze hands along a silky rope, Kelly Akashi communicates a lexicon of precise gestures like those of angels in a Flemish painting. The young Los Angeles-based artist also makes delicate blown-glass vessels which record the trace of the body in the form of exhaled breath. Akashi's hands are lively in their detachment from the body: by contrast the partial bodies sculpted by Berlinde De Bruyckere are freighted with mortality: amputated, mutilated hunks of flesh lacking limbs or heads, an almost unbearable materialisation of physical and emotional pain.

Hayv Kahraman, a Kurdish artist who fled Iraq with her family at the age of eleven, paints fragmented figures which express the particular pain of the dispossessed: '[...] detaching their limbs, for me, is very reminiscent of the psyche of a refugee, and that sense of detachment you have from your land that you've had to leave behind. That's the idea of the diasporic women, who are fragmented, or cyborgs almost. They've had to give up part of themselves.'[10] Her doll-like figures refer to the tradition of Persian miniatures as well as to the surrealist mannequin: open mouths, one with poised pink tongue, seem lasciviously offered, but are in fact derived from the pictograms used by US soldiers to direct body cavity searches on Iraqis.

The body is capable of extremes of pleasure as well as pain, of course. The icy porcelain wreaths in Rachel Kneebone's sculptures may strike a funerary note, but the piling of tangled limbs upon fruit and flower contradicts this in orgiastic abundance. Kicking limbs with delicately sculpted feet, arched ecstatically, emerge from a froth of porcelain amongst ripely suggestive folds and orbs. Pushing her medium to its limits, her works are finely balanced between form and formlessness, perfection threatening to collapse into chaos.

Dualities are at play, as so often in Bourgeois' work, in *Breasts and Blade* (1991), a reclining form suggesting an odalisque but composed of pillowy breasts. Secreted in its base, a knife blade can swing out behind. 'Sometimes I am totally concerned with female shapes', she explained, 'clusters of breasts like clouds – but often I merge that imagery – phallic breasts, male and female, active and passive. [...] My Femme-Couteau embodies the polarity of woman, the destructive and the defensive. [...] In the Femme-Couteau, the woman turns into a blade, she is defensive. She identifies with the penis to defend herself.'[11]

9. Alina Szapocznikow, *Sculpture Undone 1955–1972*, eds. Elena Filipovic and Joanna Mytkowska, Museum of Modern Art, New York, 2012.
10. Nina Siegaljan, 'Dark Memories of War Illuminate an Artist's Work', *The New York Times*, November 2013.
11. Louise Bourgeois, *New York*, 11 February 1974.

Rosemarie Trockel

Rosemarie Trockel was born in 1952 in Schwerte, Germany and studied at the Fachhochschule, Cologne. She has had major exhibitions at Museum of Modern Art, New York (1988); Museum of Contemporary Art Chicago (1991); Institute of Contemporary Art, Boston (1991); and Museum Ludwig Köln, Cologne (2005), among others. Recent solo exhibitions include 'A Cosmos', Museo Nacional de Arte Reina Sofia, Madrid (2012), touring to New York and London; 'Flagrant Delight', Wiels, Brussels (2012), touring to Lisbon and Bolzano, Italy; and 'Märzôschnee ûnd Wiebôrweh sand am Môargô niana më', Kunsthaus Bregenz, Austria (2015). She participated in Documenta 10 and 14 (1997, 2012) and was the first women to represent Germany at the 48th Venice Biennale (1999).

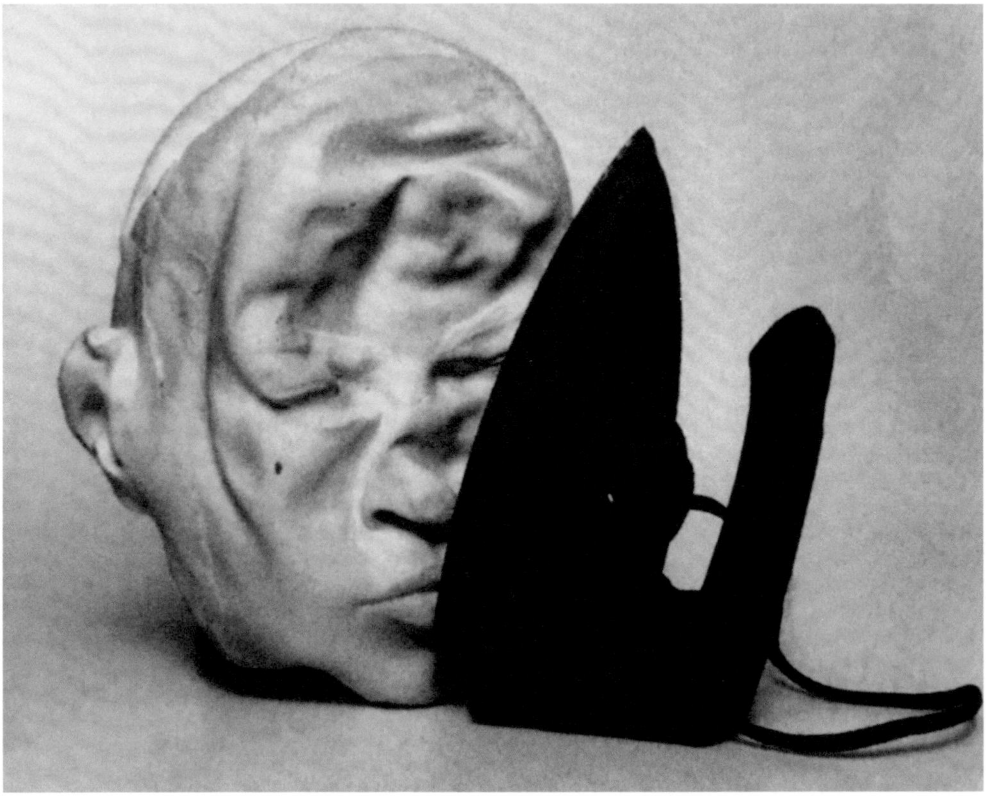

Untitled
1990/2016
Digital print
40 x 35 cm

Kelly Akashi

Kelly Akashi was born in 1983 in Los Angeles, where she lives and works. She studied at Otis College of Art and Design, Los Angeles; the Städelschule, Frankfurt am Main; and the University of Southern California, Los Angeles. Akashi has had solo exhibitions at Tomorrow Gallery, New York (2015) and Ghebaly Gallery, Los Angeles (2016). Recent group exhibitions include Hammer Museum, Los Angeles; David Roberts Art Foundation, London; Astrup Fearnley Museum of Modern Art, Oslo; The Jewish Museum, New York (all 2016); and Musée d'art contemporain de Lyon (2017).

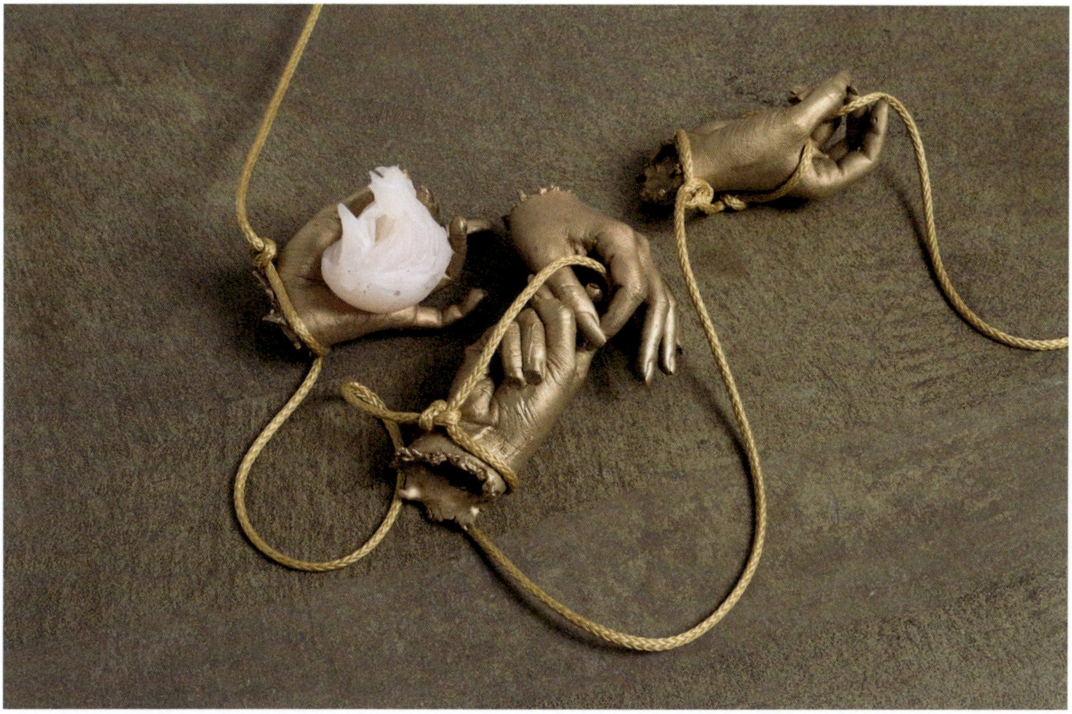

Well(-)Hung
2017
Bronze, rope and silicone
Dimensions variable

Berlinde De Bruyckere

Berlinde De Bruyckere was born in 1964 in Ghent, Belgium, where she lives and works. Uncannily realistic, her sculptures emphasise the significance of flesh as a foundation for human existence and experience, and appear to be in a state of metamorphosis. Recent solo exhibitions include Gemeentemuseum Den Haag, The Hague (2015) and 'Suture', Leopold Museum, Vienna (2016). Recent group exhibitions include 'The Importance of Being…', Museo de Arte Contemporáneo, Buenos Aires (2015); 'Flesh', York Art Gallery (2016); and 'Intuition', Palazzo Fortuny, Venice (2017). She represented Belgium at the 55th Venice Biennale (2013) and in 2015 was awarded an honorary doctorate from the University of Ghent.

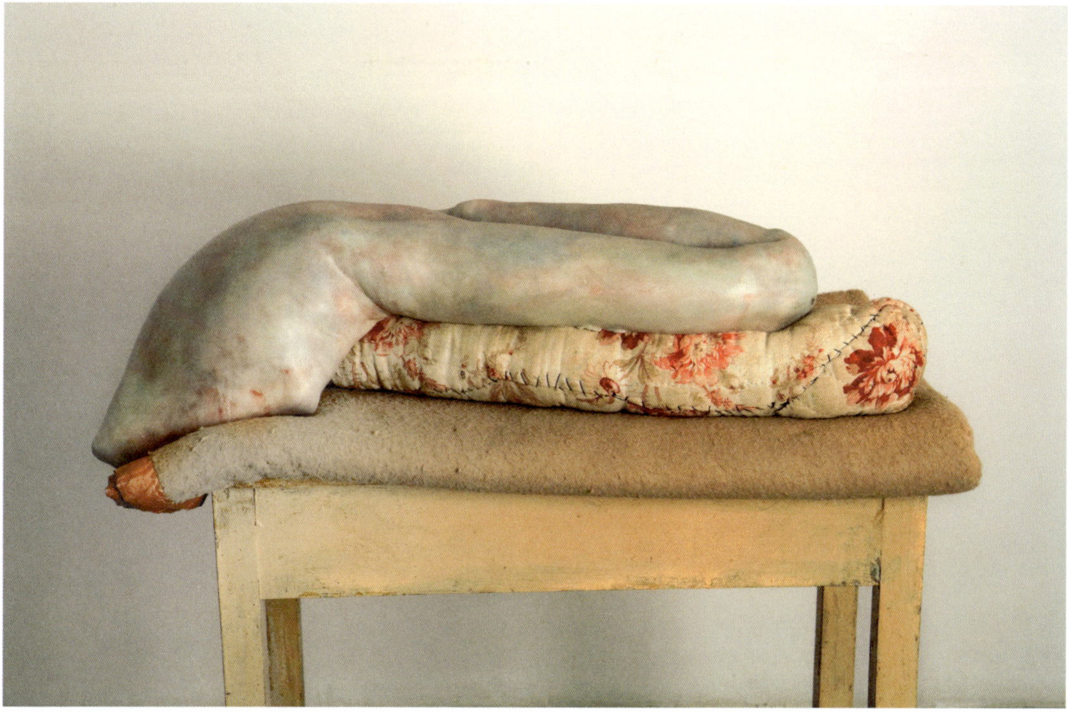

Amputeren zei je
2008
Wooden table, wax and blanket
99 x 80 x 55 cm

Hayv Kahraman

Hayv Kahraman was born in 1981 in Baghdad, Iraq, and currently lives and works in Los Angeles. Her work grapples with the marginal spaces between Western and Middle Eastern culture, as well as the aesthetics and concepts of gender through her experience as an Iraqi émigré first in Europe and then the US. Kahraman has had solo exhibitions at Third Line, Dubai (2012); Jack Shainman Gallery, New York (2015); and Joslyn Art Museum, Omaha (2016). Recent group exhibitions include 'Contemporary Narratives from Turkey and Beyond', Istanbul Modern (2014); 'Us Is Them', Pizzuti Collection, Columbus, Ohio (2015); and 'Making Her Mark', Mattatuck Museum, Waterbury, Connecticut (2016).

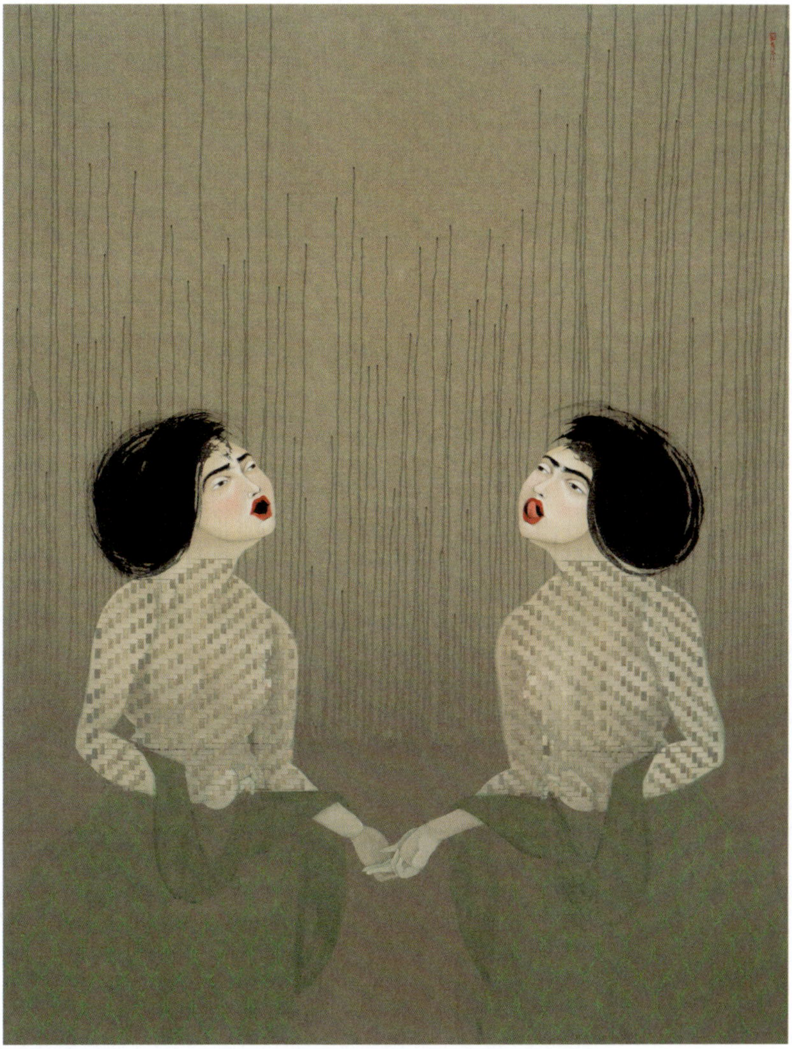

T25 and T26
2017
Oil on linen
203.2 x 152.4 cm

Rachel Kneebone

Rachel Kneebone was born in 1973 in Oxfordshire, UK, and lives and works in London. Recent solo exhibitions include 'Regarding Rodin', Brooklyn Museum, New York (2012); '399 Days', White Cube, London (2014); and 'Rachel Kneebone at the V&A', Victoria and Albert Museum, London (2017). She has participated in the group exhibitions 'The Surreal House', Barbican Art Gallery, London; 'The Beauty of Distance', 17th Biennale of Sydney (both 2010); 1st Kiev Biennale Arsenale, Ukraine (2012); '3am: Wonder, Paranoia and the Restless Night', The Bluecoat, Liverpool and Chapter, Cardiff (2013); and 'Ceramix', Bonnefantenmuseum, Maastricht (2015), among others. In 2005, Kneebone was nominated for the MaxMara Art Prize.

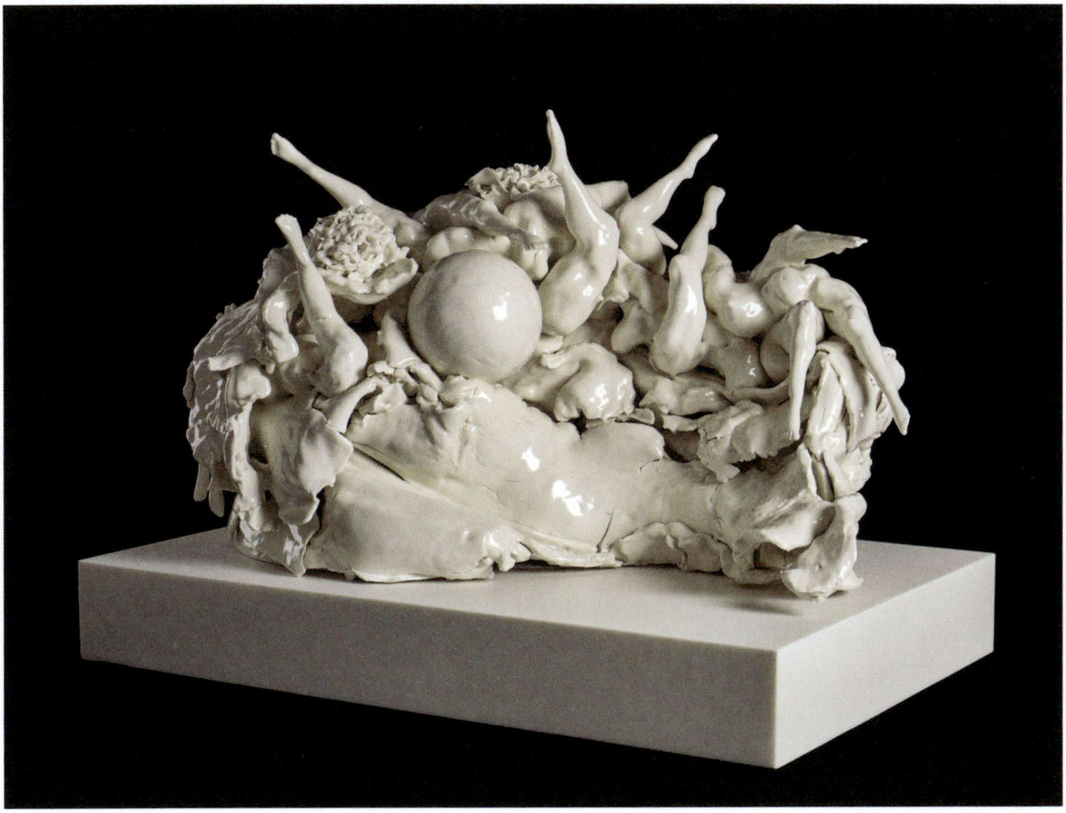

The Area on Whose Brink Silence Begins
2015
Porcelain
54 x 76 x 52 cm

Louise Bourgeois

Louise Bourgeois (1911–2010) was born in Paris and, after studying at the Sorbonne and École des Beaux-Arts, emigrated to New York in 1938. She encountered the Surrealists in both Paris and New York but never formally joined their group, instead adopting a rebellious approach, which placed women as the subject, rather than object, of her work. Bourgeois's first retrospective was shown at the Museum of Modern Art, New York, in 1982 and she has been the subject of major museum exhibitions during her lifetime and since her death. Recent solo exhibitions include 'I Have Been to Hell and Back', Moderna Museet, Stockholm (2015), touring to Museo Picasso, Malaga; 'Structures of Existence', Louisiana Museum of Modern Art, Humlebaek (2016); and 'Twosome', Tel Aviv Museum of Art (2017). Louise Bourgeois received a number of significant awards and honours in her lifetime, including the Golden Lion at the 48th Venice Biennale (1999); the Praemium Imperiale (1999); and the Ordre national de la Légion d'honneur (2008).

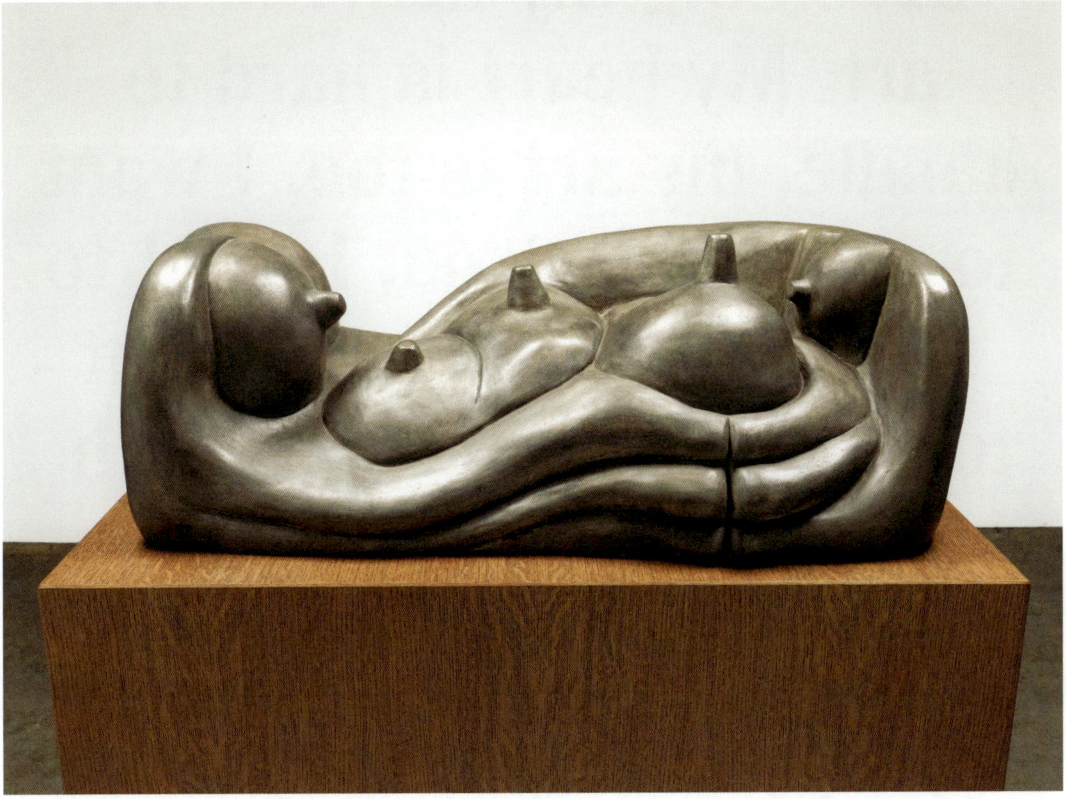

Breasts and Blade
1991
Bronze, silver nitrate and polished patina
27.9 x 81.3 x 40.6 cm

I become my art, my art becomes me. My art is becoming my heart in my art. My heart is hard to handle, my art is too. I want to overwhelm you. I want to touch your feelings I want to give you tender strength. Feel! Feel the folds; one fold, two folds, expressive precise gestural symbols. Multi-layered metaphysics below the gut level, like laughter, making love, or shaking hands.[12]

The infusion of narrative and subjectivity into the post-minimalist art of the late-1960s and '70s was identified both with the feminine and with Surrealism. As American poet Eduardo Roditi reported in 1966, 'it is the sexual content of Surrealist art and its unique dependence on the human body [...] that has performed this miracle of raising Surrealism from the dead to triumph like an avenging angel over the routed hordes of abstraction.'[13] Surrealism had already disintegrated the solid, closed body of historic sculpture. A generation including Eva Hesse, Lee Bontecou, Hannah Wilke and Louise Bourgeois brought a new gendered perspective to the discourse of the body inherited from the Surrealists, with an art shuttling between abstraction and figuration and introducing tactility, amorphousness and impermanence to sculpture. Wilke's work was intimately bound to her body. She pioneered a formal language centring on vaginal forms: folding, containing shapes implying viscera, orifice and skin, taken off the pedestal or plinth and placed on the ground. *The Five Androgynous and Vaginal Sculptures* (1960–61) are among her earliest terracotta sculptures and earliest representations of the vagina. The androgynous element is suggested by their phallic nubs and protrusions, while the secreted interiors of course suggest the feminine, not just as representation but also, by association, with a domestic function, as vessel, lamp or votive.

Maria Bartuszová, born in Prague in 1936, worked in relative isolation behind the Iron Curtain. She was reaching toward a new haptic language in sculpture while her Polish contemporary Szapocznikow was making her own revolution in sculpture in Paris. A rare venture into bronze, her *Rebound Torso* (1984) recalls Callis' image of flesh under restraint. The fragility of the plaster that is Bartuszová's usual material suggests a state of flux and impermanence, while her tactile organic forms evoke natural forces of gravity, budding, ripening and decay. Though her forms tend to abstraction, sculpture for her too sprang closely from the body, its sensations and processes: 'shapes themselves have strong psychological expressions – touching round shapes can create the feeling of a tender touch, an embrace, maybe even erotic feelings'.[11] The title of Siobhán Hapaska's *Touch* (2016) makes explicit its haptic appeal. A new material (concrete cloth, developed to provide disaster shelters) allows drapery to stand self-supported, exposing a soft furred lining. With organic meeting high-tech, and abstract forms interacting in ways that suggest narrative, Hapaska's sculpture engenders the sense of simultaneous strangeness and familiarity that characterises the surreal.

Wilke's candid, affirming expression of female sexuality aspires to universality through the association of woman, sexuality, creativity and the forces of nature. To the British Surrealist Ithell Colquhoun these associations had a mystical, occult dimension. The quest for a higher level of consciousness and the communion with greater forces of the universe ultimately led Colquhoun from Surrealism to occultism and Celticism, as in Grace Pailthorpe's case, who moved from Surrealism to Eastern mysticism, and for Penny Slinger who embraced Tantra. Generations later, Loie Hollowell's semi-abstract paintings spring from a Surrealist lineage by way of Chicago imagism. Geometric forms in low relief resolve into yoni, lingam, lip, breast and orifice, making visible a world of pulsing, celebratory sexual energy.

12. Hannah Wilke from 'Letter to Women Artists', in *Hannah Wilke Sculpture 1960s–80s*, Alison Jacques Gallery, London, 2014.
13. Eduardo Roditi, 'Letter from Paris: Surrealism Resurrected', *Apollo*, vol.83, no.5, May 1966.

Hannah Wilke

Hannah Wilke (1940–1993) was born in New York and trained at Stella Elkins Tyler School of Fine Art, Temple University, Philadelphia. She first exhibited her terracotta sculptures of vaginal forms in 1967 and had key solo museum exhibitions at Fine Arts Gallery, University of California, Irvine (1976) and University of Missouri (1989). Since her death, major solo presentations of her work include 'Intra-Venus', a US touring exhibition that opened at Ronald Feldman Fine Arts, New York (1994) and 'Gestures', Neuberger Museum of Art, New York (2008). Wilke has contributed to a large number of significant group exhibitions, including 'Naked Before the Camera', The Metropolitan Museum of Art, New York (2012); 'The Original Copy: Photography of Sculpture, 1839 to Today', Museum of Modern Art, New York (2010); and 'elles@centre-pompidou', Centre Pompidou, Paris, 2010.

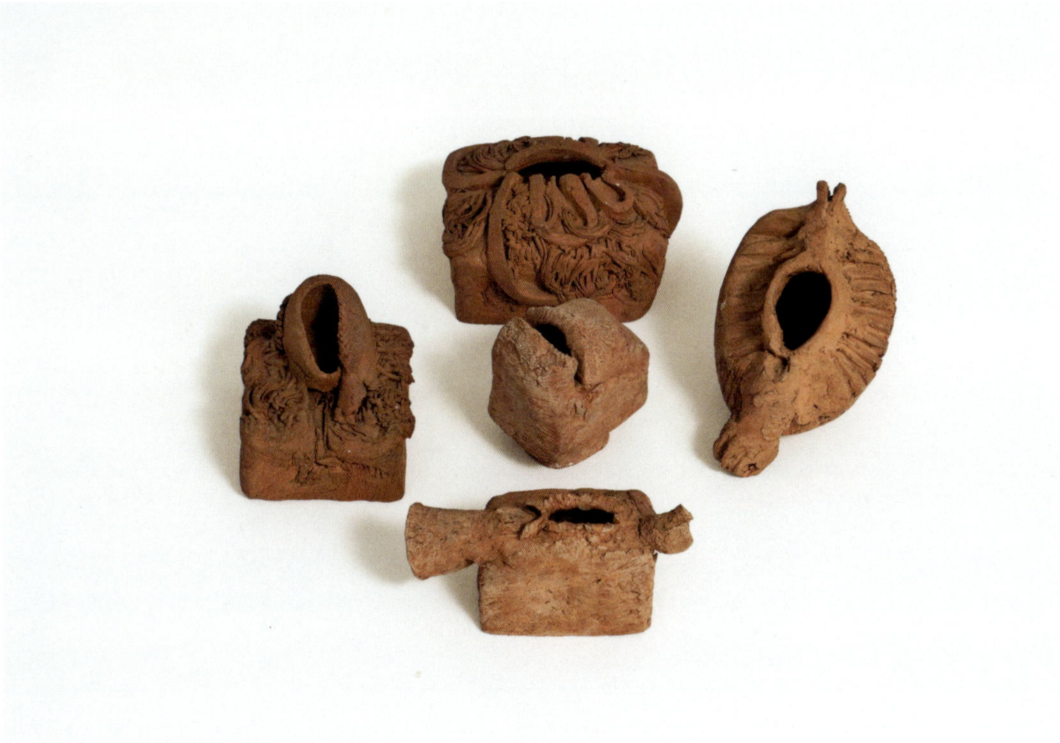

Five Androgynous and Vaginal Sculptures
1960–61
Terracotta
Dimensions variable

Maria Bartuszová

Maria Bartuszová (1936–96) was born in Prague, where she studied at the Academy of Applied Arts, graduating in 1961. Bartuszová spent much of her life in the city of Košice, in eastern Slovakia, where she developed her experimental method of casting plaster using rubber balloons and tubes, inspired by the modernist forms of Constantin Brâncuşi and Henry Moore. Since her death, Bartuszová has been the subject of solo exhibitions in London (2016), Warsaw and Munich (both 2014). Recent group exhibitions include 'Disobedient Bodies', The Hepworth Wakefield (2017); 'Desire for Freedom: Art in Europe since 1945', Deutsches Historisches Museum, Berlin (2012); and 'Gender Check', MUMOK, Vienna (2010).

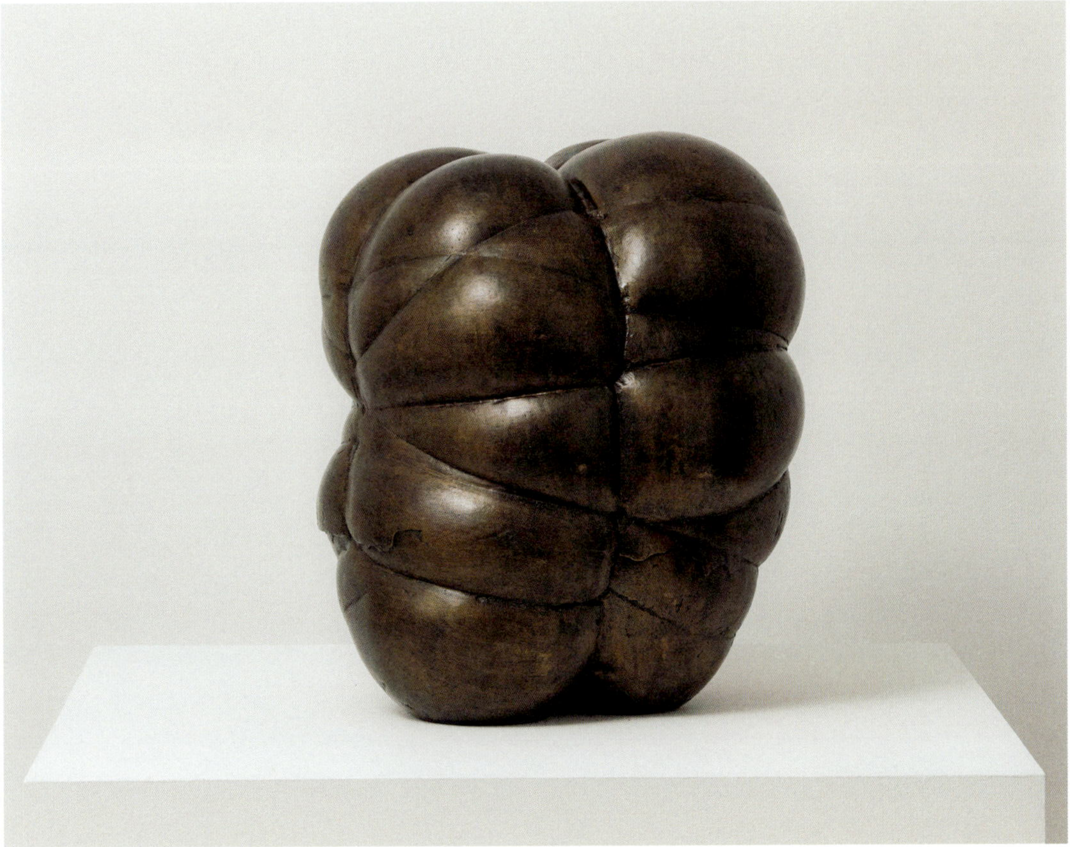

Rebound Torso
1984
Vintage bronze
42 x 33 x 32 cm

Siobhán Hapaska

Siobhán Hapaska was born in 1963 in Belfast and lives and works in London. At the core of Hapaska's work is a consideration of human relations and conflicting ideologies. Recent solo exhibitions include Camden Arts Centre, London (2007); Magasin III, Stockholm (2013); and Museum Boijmans Van Beuningen, Rotterdam (2015). Hapaska took part in Documenta 10 (1997) and represented Ireland at the 49th Venice Biennale (2001).

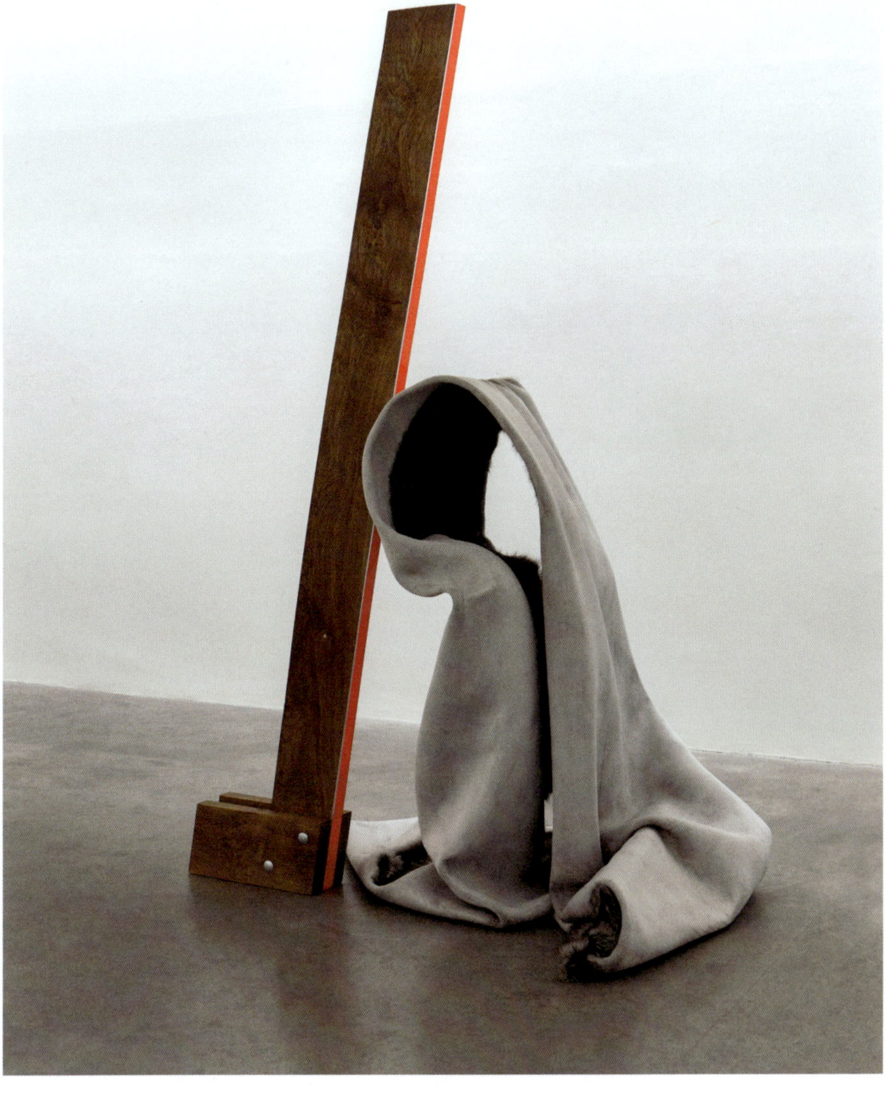

Touch
2016
Concrete cloth, oak, synthetic fur, aluminium, steel, two-pack acrylic paint and lacquer
230 x 95 x 140 cm

Ithell Colquhoun

Ithell Colquhoun (1906–88) was born in Assam, India and attended the Slade School of Art in 1928. She travelled extensively in Europe in the 1930s and met André Breton in 1939, the same year that she joined the Surrealist Group in England and contributed to its journal, *London Bulletin*. Her interest in the occult led to her split from the group in the early 1940s, at which time her work began to explore the unconscious, through automatism, Dali's 'double image' and decalcomania. Colquhoun moved to Cornwall in 1957, from where she published her writing and continued to live until her death. Recent group exhibitions include 'Angels of Anarchy, Manchester Art Gallery; 'British Surrealism in Context', Leeds City Art Gallery (both 2009); and 'Watercolours', Tate Britain, London (2011).

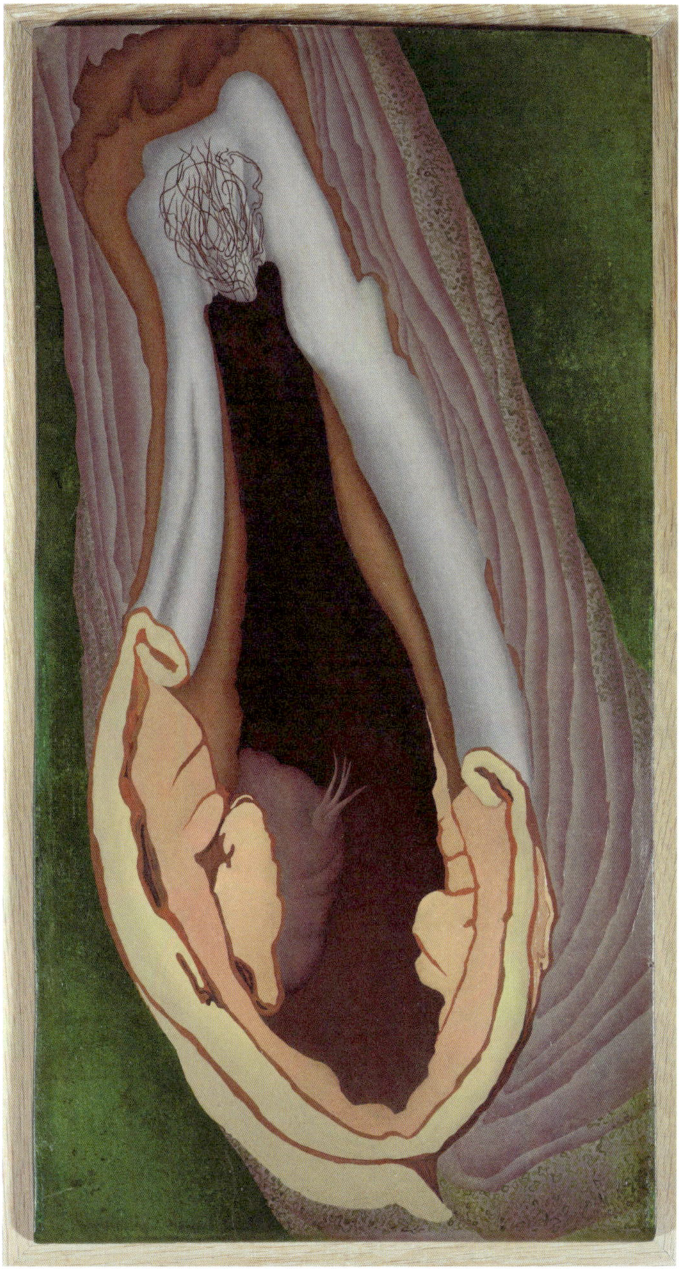

Tree Anatomy
1942
Oil on panel
56.9 x 29 cm

Loie Hollowell

Loie Hollowell was born in 1983 in Woodland, California and lives and works in New York. She attended the University of California, Santa Barbara, and Virginia Commonwealth University. Originating in autobiography her paintings explore themes of sexuality, often through abstractions of the human body and allusions to iconography such as the almond-shaped mandorlas found in medieval religious painting. Hollowell was the recipient of a 2011 Virginia Museum of Fine Arts Fellowship Award.

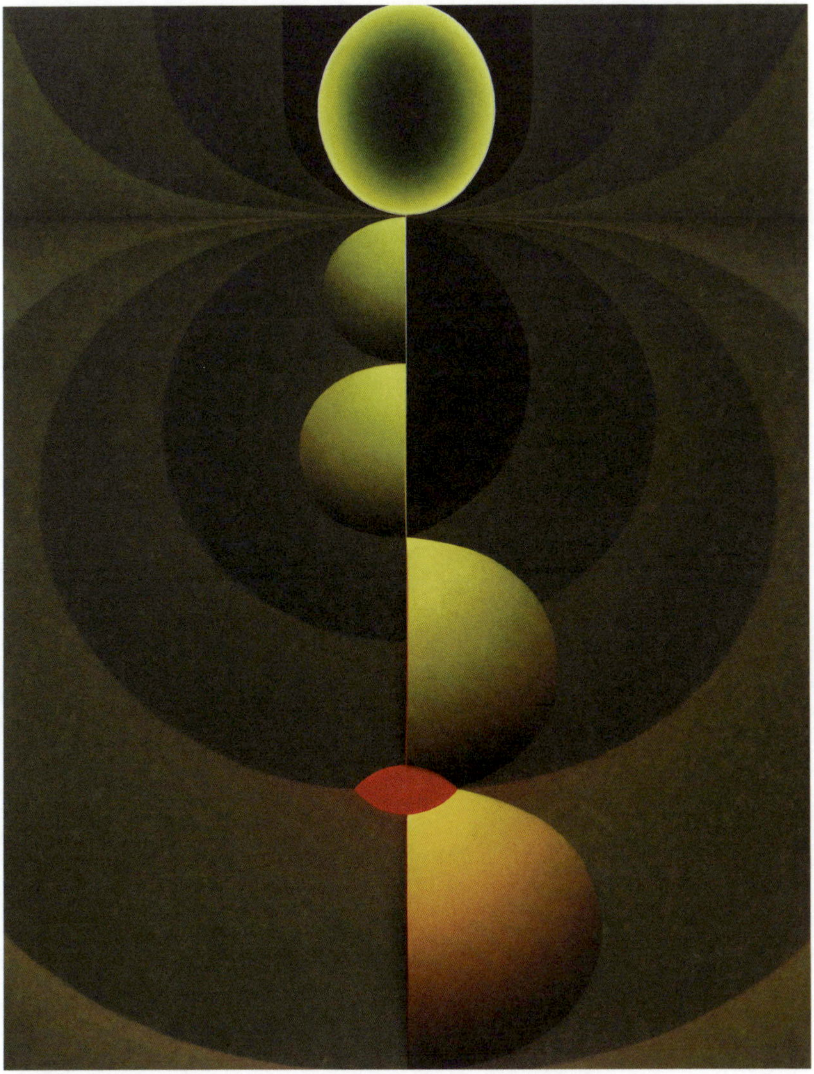

Full Frontal
2016
Oil, acrylic, sawdust and high density foam on linen over panel
91.4 x 121.9 cm

‘Outer and inner eye, backward and forward, inside out and upside down, sideways, as a metaphysical airplane might go.’ [14]

The Surrealists' great enterprise was to unlock the power of the unconscious mind, wherein they believed true creativity resided. In this, the recently published writings of Freud were a major inspiration. Gabriella Boyd has drawn subjects from the case studies recorded in Freud's *Interpretation of Dreams* to create enigmatic images, as lucid, bright and fragmentary as dream memories. One of the most enthusiastic explorers of the unconscious was Dr Grace Pailthorpe, a psychoanalyst hailed by André Breton as 'the best and most truly Surrealist' of artists, though her membership of the British Surrealist movement was short-lived. Breton's stint as a medic in an army mental hospital during World War I had fed his own fascination with the creativity unlocked in those disinhibited by psychiatric disturbance, and his novel *Nadja* (1928) recounts his brief, intoxicating fascination with a disturbed young woman. Working today, Czech artist Eva Kot'átková uses strategies of collage and performance developed by the Surrealists to create dense, absurdist psychological dramas relating to confinement and oppression. Fascinated by mental illness and those outside society's norms, like the Surrealists, she also draws on dreams and children's drawings in her imagery.

For many artists, mental illness was something experienced more intimately than as a scientific observer, as it was for Carol Rama when in 1933, at the impressionable age of fifteen, she saw her mother admitted to a psychiatric clinic. Fascinated by the behaviour of female patients who wandered the wards half naked, the artist began her 'vulgar' drawings. Often depicting women restrained or confined, yet defiantly sexual, they express the resistance of the body to dominating, normalising forces that implicates the restrictive patriarchal culture of fascist Italy. 'I paint to heal myself', Rama said, a sentiment echoed by Bourgeois: 'Art is a guarantee of sanity. That is the most important thing I have said', and 'Art is restoration: the idea is to repair the damages that are inflicted in life, to make something that is fragmented – which is what fear and anxiety do to a person – into something whole.' The Surrealists acknowledged the difficulty of making truly automatic painting, since all painting, especially figurative, requires deliberation and choice. Some artists, including the young painters Gabriella Boyd and Issy Wood, describe efforts to work with an urgency or detachment that tricks the controlling, rational brain to relinquish control and allows images to surface from unknown depths. Whilst one approach is to attempt to channel the unconscious mind in the creation of the work, another is to trigger responses deep in the viewer's own unconscious by the considered use of imagery and juxtaposition. Dreams, allegory, fable and fairy tales are other means of accessing the universal truths and experiences of the subconscious, speaking to us from a powerful reserve of common understanding. Leonora Carrington, herself confined and forcibly treated in a Spanish asylum after her separation from Max Ernst, fled to Mexico City, the nation Breton called the most surreal on earth. She drew on Mayan, astrological and mystical imagery for her strange landscapes full of feathered and fishy hybrids. Paloma Varga Weisz's enigmatic tableaux trigger a sense of recognition that seems half-dreamt, half-remembered. The imagery of the centuries is layered with fragments of narrative and human-animal hybrids, making the domestic seem wondrous and uncanny.

Tomoko Kashiki's work also conflates the contemporary and archaic, borrowing from Heian Buddhist paintings and the Bijinga school of paintings of women of her home city of Kyoto. She paints young women trapped in a treacherous architecture of liquefying solids and dissolving perspective. Sascha Braunig's meticulously rendered figures appear to exist in another alien environment, where they are stretched, compressed, twisted or irradiated by a sickly glow. As if taking on protective camouflage, or somehow leaching out beyond the body's boundaries, they seem to merge with their environment. The heavy-limbed figures that crowd the frame of Jordan Kasey's paintings inhabit a world of syrupy light and extreme gravity; forms melt and bubble in the rays that shaft through Cheyenne Julien's shadowy architecture. These worlds each have their own laws of physics, their own logic – the irrational logic of a dream. We feel for their inhabitants who, like Alice, stretching and shrinking in wonderland, are influenced by forces beyond their control.

---

14. Eileen Agar, 'Am I A Surrealist?', in *Surrealist Women*, ed. Penelope Rosemont, Bloomsbury, London, 1998.

Eileen Agar

Eileen Agar RA (1899–1991) was born in Buenos Aires to Scottish and American parents and was educated in England from 1911. She studied at the Slade School of Art in London before moving to Paris in 1928, where she met and befriended André Breton and Paul Éluard. In the 1930s, Agar exhibited with the Surrealists in London, Paris and New York and was inspired by the visual metaphors of her contemporaries – their 'interpenetrating of reason and unreason'. Her work has been included in the group exhibitions 'The Art of Assemblage', Museum of Modern Art, New York (1961) and 'British Surrealism & Other Realities', Middlesbrough Institute of Modern Art (2008), as well as the inaugural display at Tate Modern (2000). Agar was elected a Royal Academician in 1990.

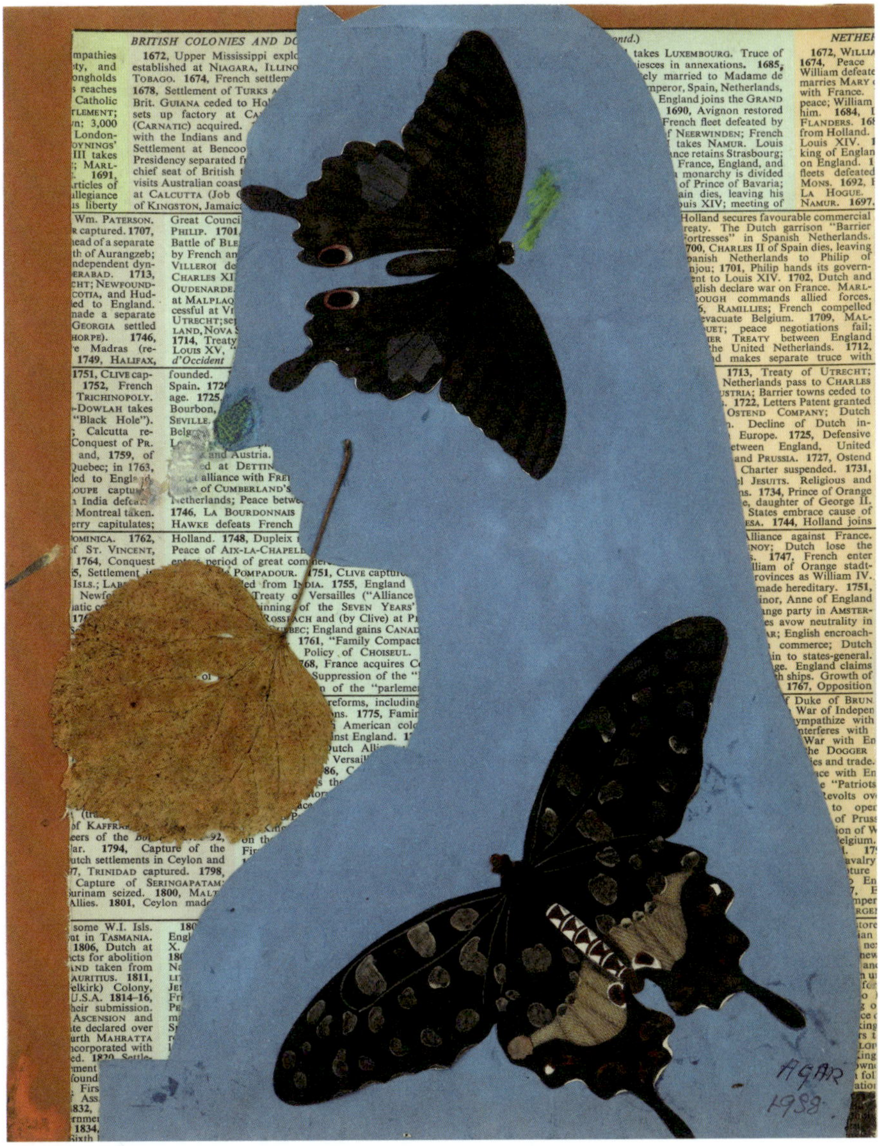

Butterfly Bride
1938
Gouache and collage
27.5 x 20.5 cm

Gabriella Boyd

Gabriella Boyd was born in 1988 in Glasgow and studied at Glasgow School of Art and the Royal Academy Schools, London. Recent exhibitions include the solo exhibition 'Strong Necks', High House Gallery, Oxford (2013) and the group exhibitions 'House for an Art Lover', Glasgow International (2016) and 'Premiums: Interim Projects', Royal Academy of Arts, London (2016). In 2015, she was commissioned to illustrate the Folio Society's new edition of Sigmund Freud's *Interpreting Dreams*.

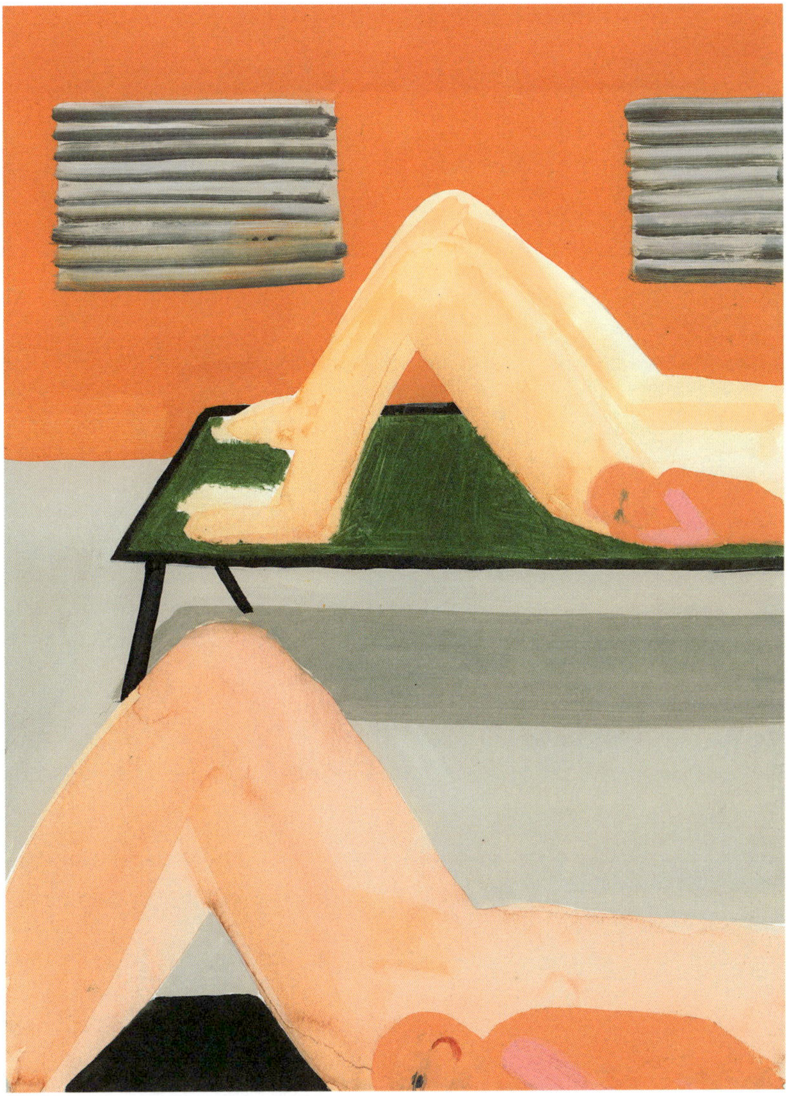

I saw two grown men lying on wooden benches against walls of the hut and two children, as it were, sleeping beside them.
2015
Watercolour and oil on paper
59 x 42 cm
Commissioned to illustrate the Folio Society's edition of Sigmund Freud's Interpretation of Dreams.

Grace Pailthorpe

Grace Pailthorpe (1883–1971) was born in Surrey, UK. After pursuing a medical degree, she served as a surgeon in the First World War. In the 1920s, Pailthorpe began to practice as a psychoanalyst and her psychoanalytic studies of female prisoners, culminating in the publication of *What We Put in Prison* (1932), drew international recognition. Together with the artist Reuben Mednikoff, Pailthorpe began to explore the role of the unconscious in painting; they were described by Andre Breton as the 'the best and most truly Surrealist' of their British contemporaries in the 1930s. Nevertheless, the two were expelled from the British Surrealist Group in 1940 for their distinctive, analytical approach and, in the subsequent decades, many of Pailthorpe's paintings were lost. Leeds City Art Gallery exhibited the first major retrospective of Pailthorpe and Mednikoff's work, 'Sluice Gates of the Mind', in 1998.

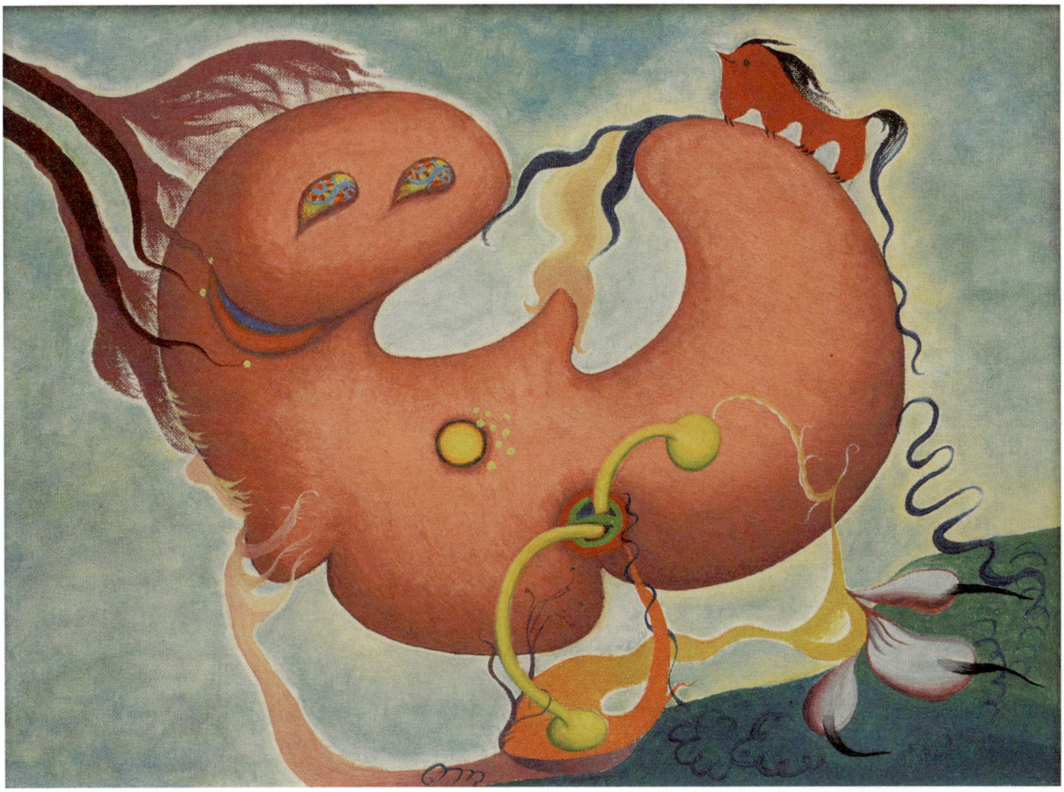

May 16th, 1941
1941
Oil on canvas board
30 x 40 cm

Eva Kot'átková

Eva Kot'átková was born in 1982 in Prague, where she lives and works. Solo exhibitions include 'A Story Teller's Inadequacy', Modern Art Oxford (2013); 'Training in Ambidexterity', Fundació Joan Miró, Barcelona (2015); and 'Room for Anxious Objects', Kunstsammlung Nordrhein-Westfalen, Düsseldorf (2017). Recent group exhibitions include 'Bedlam', Wellcome Collection, London (2016) and 'Proposals to Surrender', Ming Contemporary Art Museum, Shanghai (2017). In 2007, she became the youngest recipient of the Jindrich Chalupecky award for Czech artists and has participated in residencies in Vienna (2012), Dublin (2014) and Saché (2017).

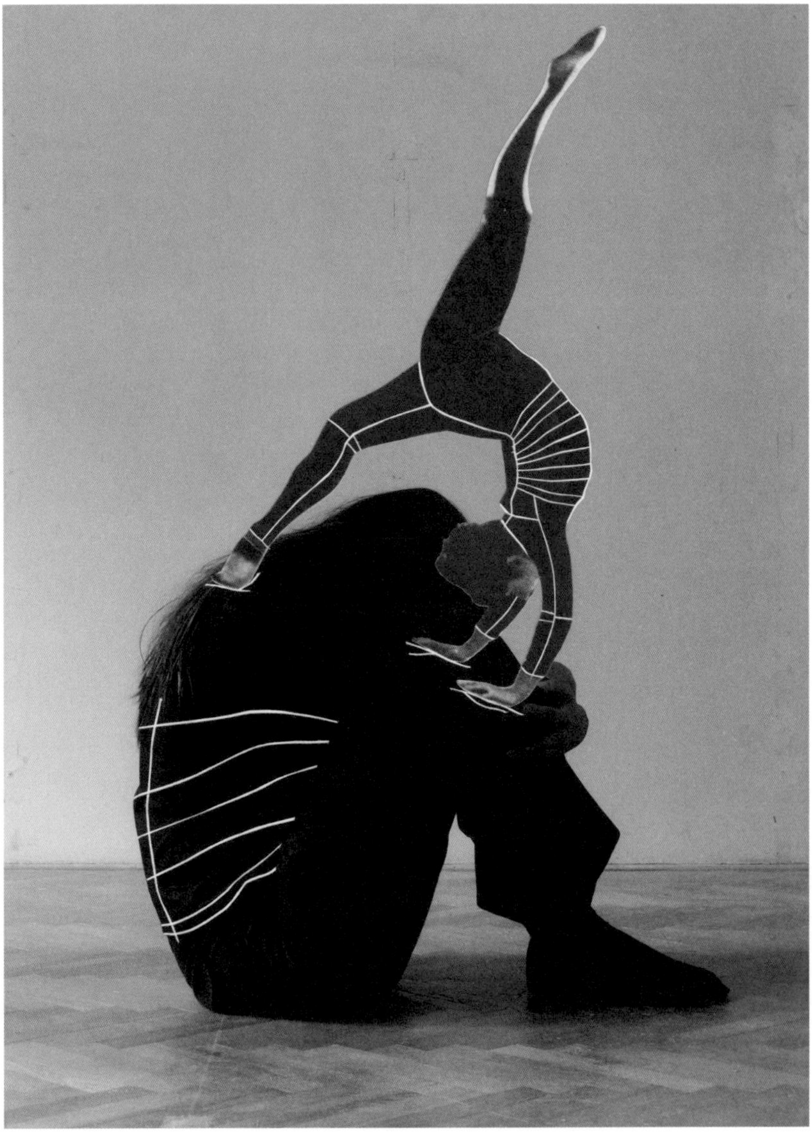

Untitled
2013
Black and white photograph combined with collage
45.5 x 35.5 cm

Carol Rama

Carol Rama (1918–2015) was born in Turin, where she lived for most of her life. Her work has been the subject of many significant solo exhibitions and retrospectives, of which recent examples include 'The Passion According to Carol Rama', Museu d'Art Contemporani de Barcelona (2015), touring to Paris, Espoo, Dublin and Turin; and 'Antibodies', New Museum, New York (2017). In 2003, she was awarded the Golden Lion for Lifetime Achievement at the 50th Venice Biennale.

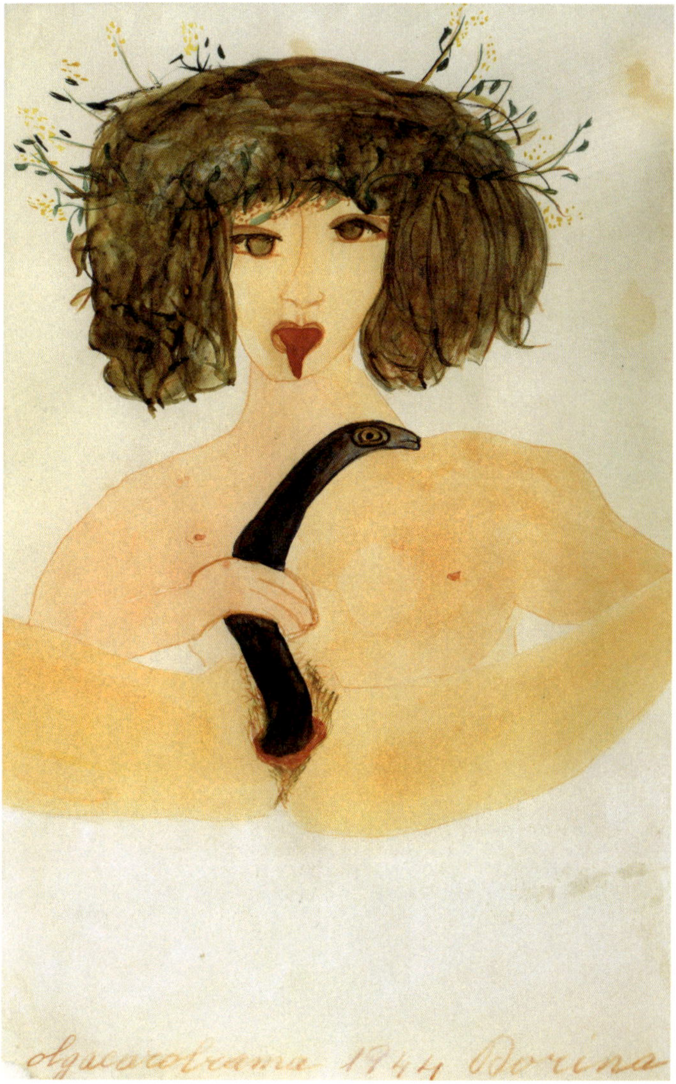

Dorina
1944
Pastel and watercolour on paper
24.5 x 15 cm

Paloma Varga Weisz

Paloma Varga Weisz was born in 1966 in Neustadt an der Weinstrasse, Germany, and lives and works in Düsseldorf. She studied at the Staatliche Kunstakademie, Düsseldorf. Major solo exhibitions include 'Spirits of My Flesh', Chapter, Cardiff (2011); 'Krummer Hund', Kabinett für aktuelle Kunst, Bremerhaven, Germany (2013), touring to Dublin; 'Roots of a Dream', Castello di Rivoli, Turin (2015); 'Kabinettstück', Fürstenberg Zeitgenössisch, Donaueschingen, Germany (2016); and Skulpturenhalle, Thomas Schütte Foundation, Holzheim, Germany (2017). Group shows include the Berlin Biennale (2006); Folkestone Triennial, UK (2011); 'The Human Factor', Hayward Gallery, London (2014); and 'Cranach', Museum Kunstpalast, Düsseldorf (2017).

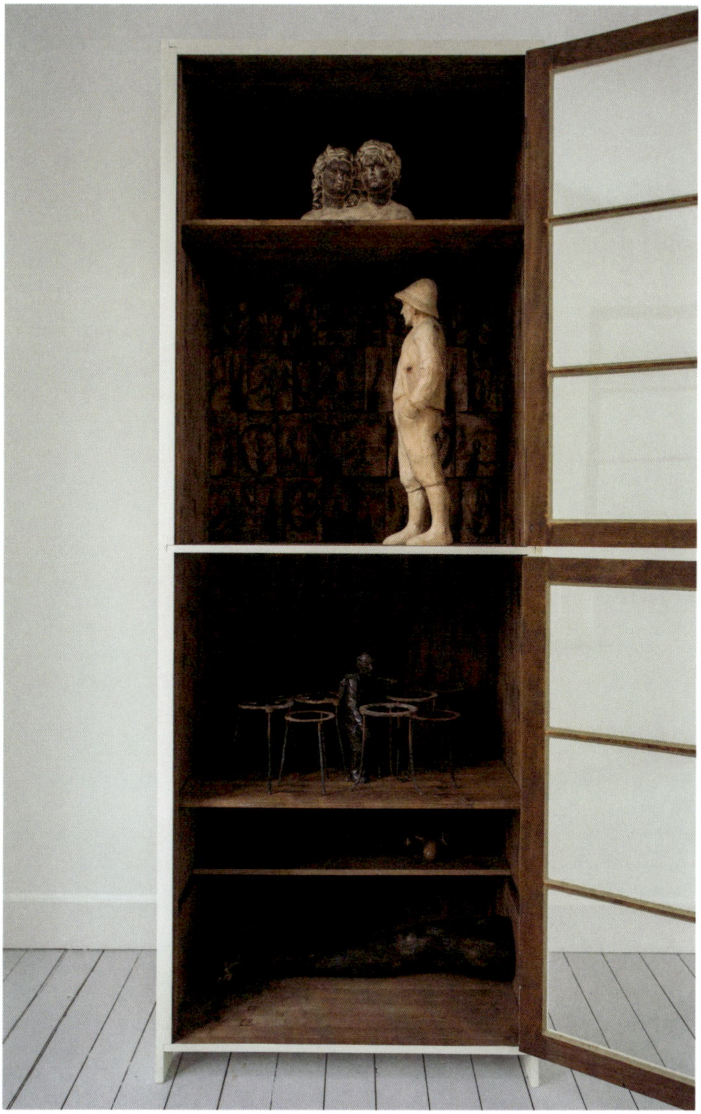

Bois Dormant – Cabinet 4
2015
Wood, glass and metal
250 x 90 x 64 cm

Tomoko Kashiki

Tomoko Kashiki was born in 1982 in Kyoto, where she lives and works. Kashiki graduated with both an MFA and PHD in painting from the Kyoto City University of Arts Graduate School. Her paintings have featured in 'Bye Bye Kitty!!!', Japan Society Gallery, New York (2011); the Yokohama Triennale (2011); and the 7th Asia Pacific Triennale of Contemporary Art (2012).

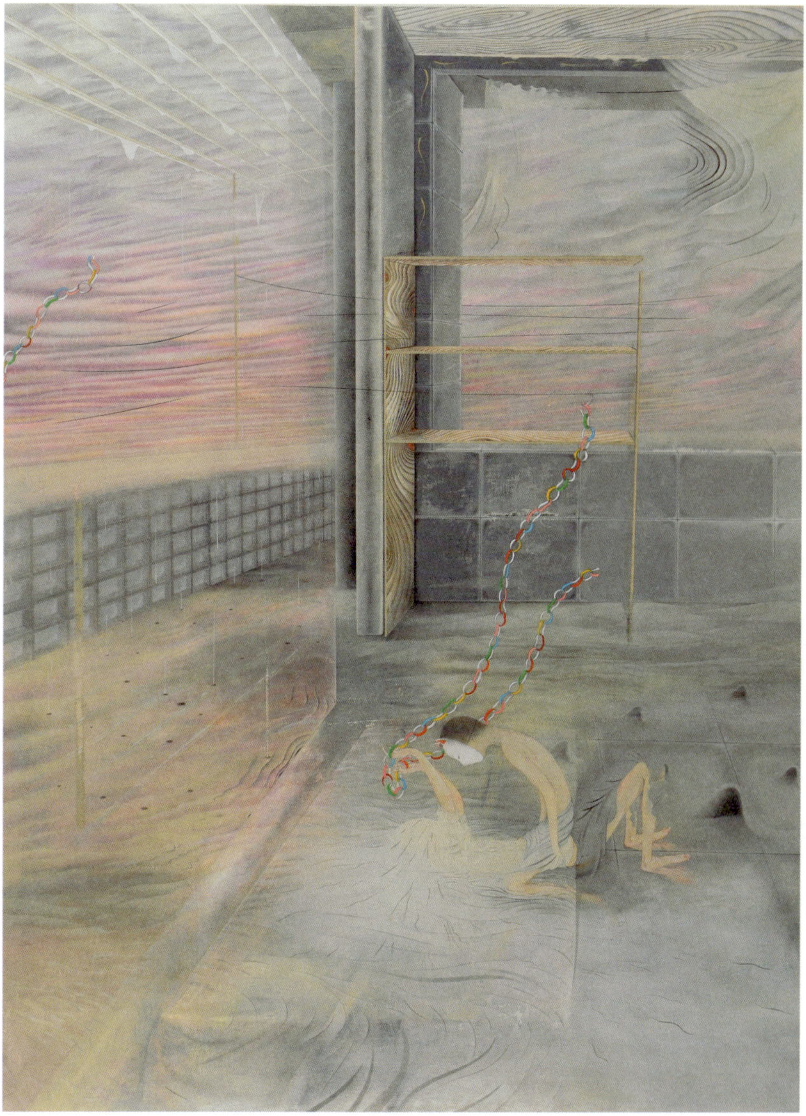

Hello Goodbye
2016
Acrylic, ink, pencil, pastel, linen and wooden panel
250 x 180 cm

Sascha Braunig

Sascha Braunig was born in 1983 in Qualicum Beach, Canada, and lives and works in Brooklyn, New York. She studied at The Cooper Union, New York, and Yale University, New Haven, Connecticut. Braunig has had solo exhibition at MoMA PS1, New York, and Kunsthall Stavanger (both 2016). Her work has been included in the group exhibitions 'A Top Hat, a Monocle, and a Butterfly', Etablissement d'en face projects, Brussels; 'Animal/Vegetable/Mineral: An Artists Guide to the World', Florence Griswold Museum, Old Lynne, Connecticut; and 'Surreal Selves', Baltimore Museum of Art (all 2013); 'Surround Audience', New Museum Triennial, New York (2015); and 'Stranger', Museum of Contemporary Art Cleveland, Ohio (2016).

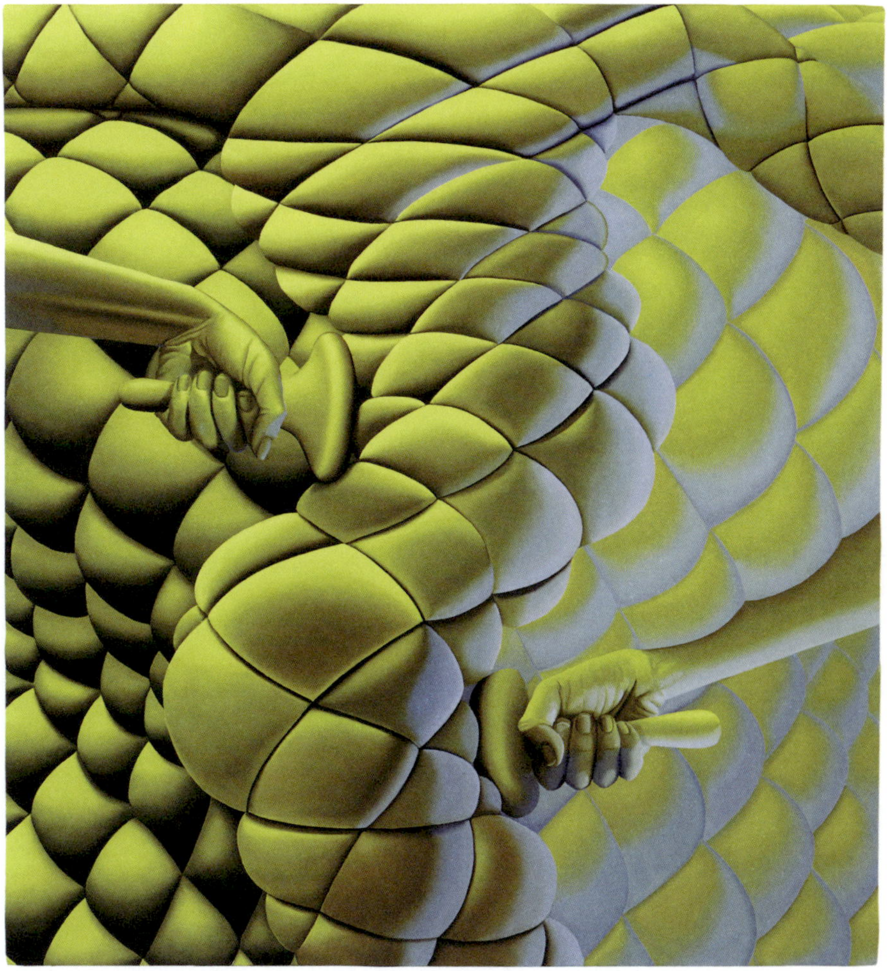

Warm Leatherette
2015
Oil on canvas over panel
67.3 x 73.7 cm

Jordan Kasey

Jordan Kasey was born in 1985 and lives and works in Brooklyn, New York. She received her BFA from the Maryland Institute College of Art. She has had solo exhibitions at Whole Gallery, Baltimore (2012); Signal Gallery, Brooklyn; Greenpoint Terminal Gallery, Brooklyn; Michael Jon Gallery, Miami (all 2015); and Nicelle Beauchene Gallery, New York (2017). Recent group exhibitions include Revue Gallery, London; Johannes Vogt, East Hampton; Thierry Goldberg Gallery, New York (all 2016); and MoMA PS1, New York (2017).

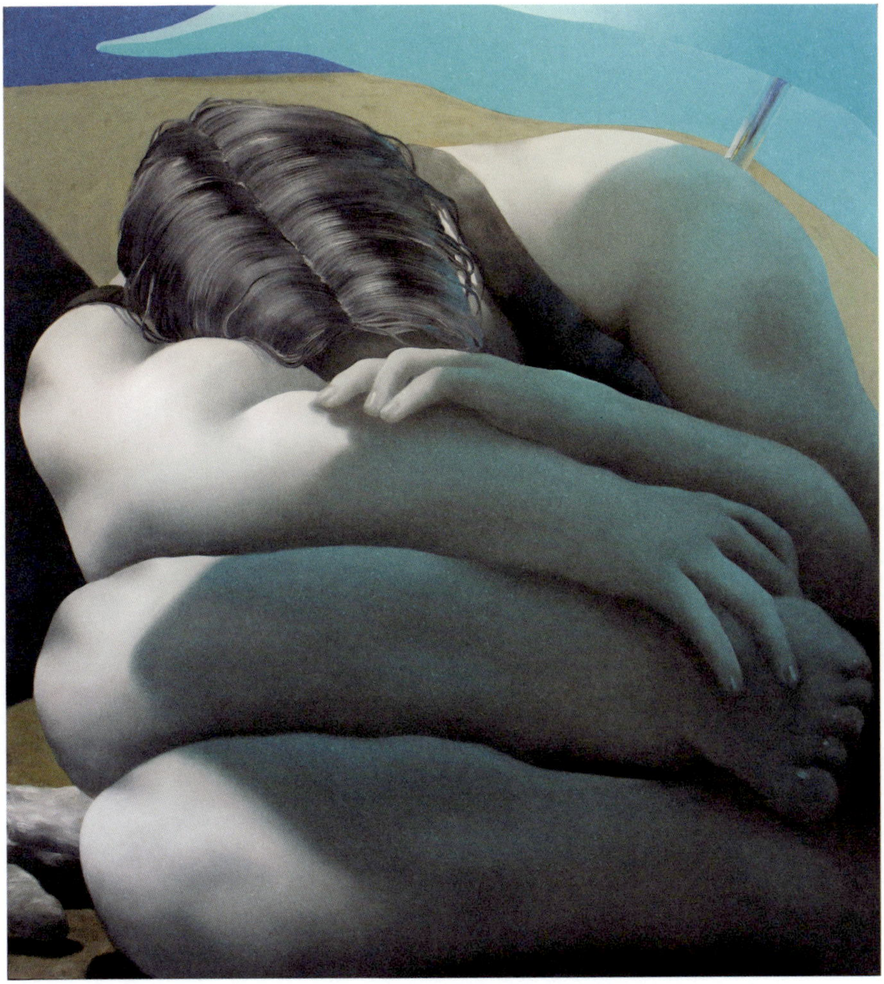

Person under a blue umbrella
2015
Oil on canvas
180.3 x 161.3 cm

Cheyenne Julien

Cheyenne Julien was born in 1994 in the Bronx, New York, where she lives and works. Julien received her BFA in Painting from the Rhode Island School of Design, where she was a recipient of the Florence Leif Award. Most recently she has participated in residencies at the Skowhegan School of Painting and Sculpture, New York, and the Ox-Bow School of Art, Napa, California.

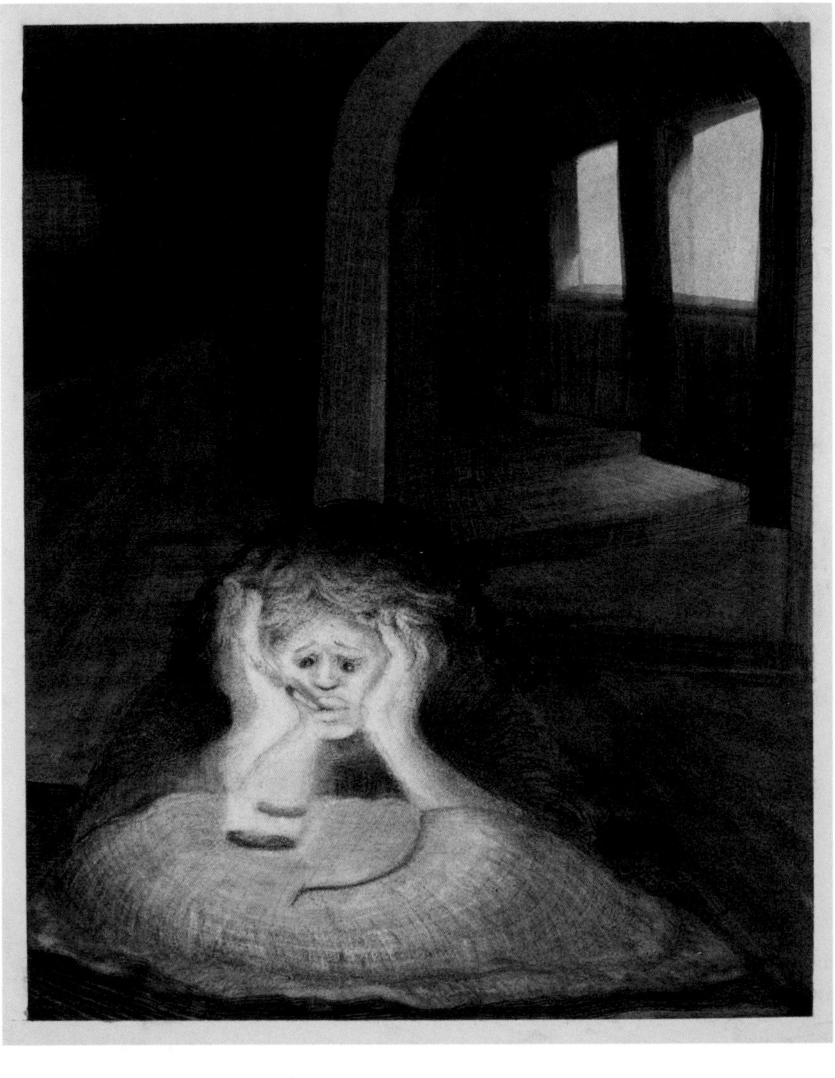

Lovers
2016
Charcoal and ink on illustration board
50.8 x 40.6 cm

‘Beneath this mask another mask. I will never finish stripping away all these faces.’[15]

Leonora Carrington's stories are full of disguises, hybrids and place-swapping. One of these occult parables, *La Debutante* (1937), deals with a macabre instance of mask-wearing. In it, a debutante avoids a high society ball by sending a hyena in her place, disguised in gloves, high heels and a mask made from the face of her maid 'nibbled very neatly all around'. At the party, and given away by its animal reek, the creature calmly devours the mask before leaping from the window.

A runaway debutante herself, Carrington was later to interrogate the constructed and culturally determined nature of womanhood in her 1970 essay 'What is A Woman', beginning 'I was born a female human animal'.[16] Some of the youngest artists in the exhibition also express a sense that 'womanliness' is a state to assume or a performance to be learned: either separate from one's true self or but a single aspect of it. Elizabeth Jaeger's earlier sculptures included discomforting, sweetly smiling nudes, informed by the observation of her college years that young women's bodies are expected to be available – to scrutiny, judgement, or touch. Here, she shows torsos that rest on metal stands, as if femininity were a state to be peeled away at will, a chrysalis from which to emerge, or (quite literally) a breastplate, donned protectively. Resting horizontally, they also read as saddles to be mounted. Femininity is shown as an ill-fitting costume in the close, musty interiors of Issy Wood's work. Witchy fake nails and hanks of hair, hand mirrors and drapes of net and velvet evoke the uncomfortable glamour of trying on your mother's high heels and lipstick, an initiation into feminity.

Claude Cahun, now celebrated as a transgender icon, rejected binary definitions of gender completely. Born Lucy Schwob, she adopted her gender-neutral name, as later the Czech Surrealist Marie Čermínová was to rename herself Toyen, for 'citoyen'. In Cahun's autobiography, *Disavowals* (1930), she wrote: 'Shuffle the cards. Masculine? Feminine? It depends on the situation. Neuter is the only gender that always suits me.' In her extraordinary photos, never exhibited in her lifetime, she dresses up as Buddha, a strongman, a pinup, Ophelia drifting in a rock pool; except when masked, her strong beaky face is unmistakeable in all its guises.

Gillian Wearing pays direct tribute to Cahun in an image recreating a self-portrait in which Cahun poses, a strange combination of masculine (leotard, circus strongman's dumbbells) and hyper feminine (kiss curls, painted pout): in her version, 'Cahun' holds a mask of the younger artist's face. Wearing disguises a doll-like Lily Cole, behind a distressed and damaged mask of the model's own features. The silicone masks she painstakingly creates are so life-like that the glimpse of the wearer's eyes through the eyeholes is deeply uncanny. Donning a mask is transformative and liberating, according to the artist: she has worn the faces of her younger self, of family members, and of her 'spiritual family' or artist heroes, as if to explore those many selves that are parts of her own self.

15. Claude Cahun in her autobiography *Disavowals or Cancelled Confessions*, trans. Susan de Muth, MIT Press, Cambridge, Massachussets, 2007.
16. Leonora Carrington, 'What is a Woman?', in The Surrealism Reader, ed. Dawn Ades and Michael Richardson with Kryzstof Fijalkowski, Tate Publishing, London, 2015.

Leonora Carrington

Leonora Carrington OBE (1917–2011) was born to an aristocratic family in Lancashire, and studied art in Florence before attending Chelsea School of Art, London. After meeting Max Ernst at a party in 1937, the two moved to Paris where Carrington became immersed in the Surrealist Group and began to explore the symbolic potential of the unconscious and natural worlds. Since her death in 2011, Carrington has been the subject of retrospectives at the Irish Museum of Modern Art, Dublin (2014) and Tate Liverpool (2015). Her work has featured in numerous group exhibitions including 'Art in Latin America', Hayward Gallery, London (1989); 'Surrealism: Desire Unbound', Tate Modern, London (2001); and 'In Wonderland', Los Angeles County Museum of Art (2012).

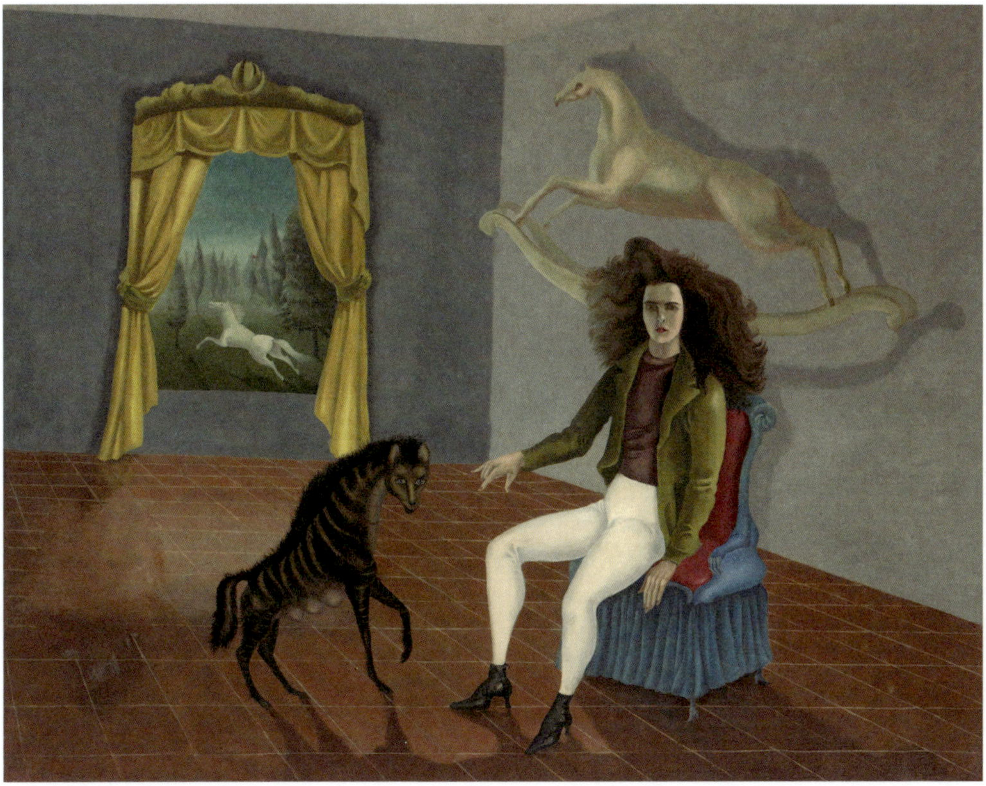

Self portrait
1937–38
Oil on canvas
65 x 81.3 cm

Elizabeth Jaeger

Elizabeth Jaeger was born in 1988 in San Francisco and lives and works in Brooklyn, New York. She has had solo exhibitions at Eli Ping, New York (2013); Jack Hanley Gallery, New York (2014, 2017); and And Now, Dallas (2015). Jaeger has participated in 'Dirty Linen', DESTE Foundation, Athens; 'Greater New York', MoMA PS1, New York; 'Fear of a Blank Pancake', White Flag Projects, St. Louis (all 2015); 'In Practice: Fantasy Can Invent Nothing New, SculptureCenter, New York; and 'Mirror Cells', Whitney Museum of American Art, New York (both 2016). Published works include *Eros C'est la Vie* (Totem, 2013); *Ships in the Night* (Peradam, 2016); and *Denude* (Peradam, 2017).

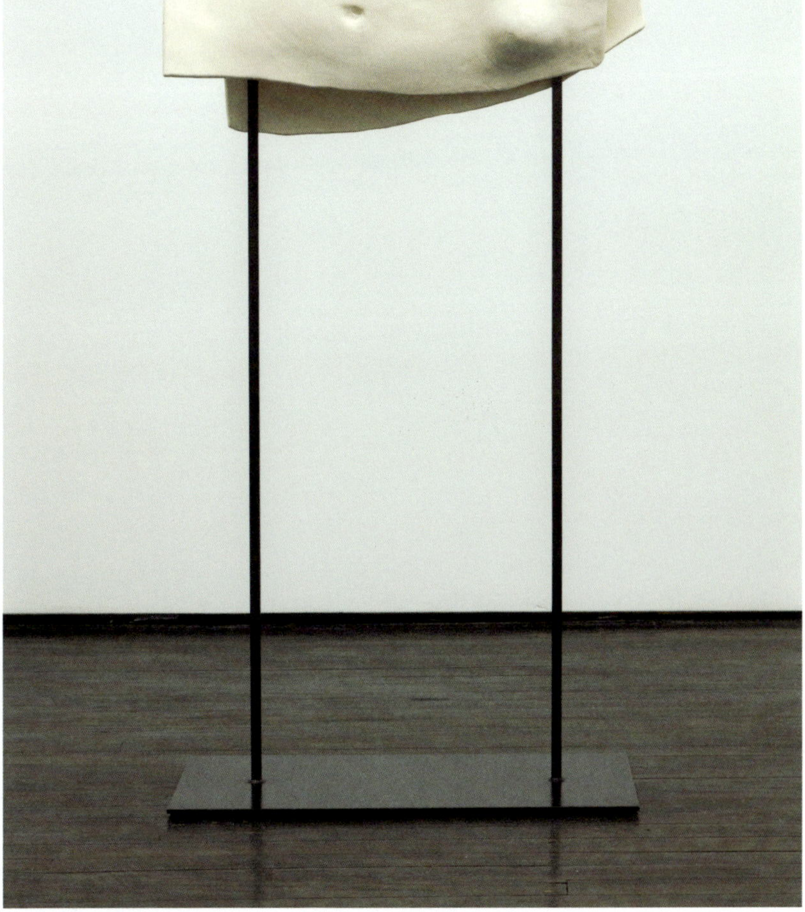

Shell
2017
Ceramic and steel
114.3 x 53.3 x 15.2 cm

Issy Wood

Issy Wood was born in 1993 in the United States and lives and works in London. She received her BA in Fine Art and History of Art from Goldsmiths in 2015 and is currently part of the Royal Academy Schools postgraduate programme. Her first solo exhibition, 'Rosetta Stone' was shown at Triumph Gallery, Moscow (2015) while recent solo exhibitions include 'All Day Breakfast', Reading International, UK (2017); 'Streams of Warm Impermanence', David Roberts Art Foundation, London (2016); and 'Chatsubo', Kraupa Tuskany Zeidler, Berlin (2016).

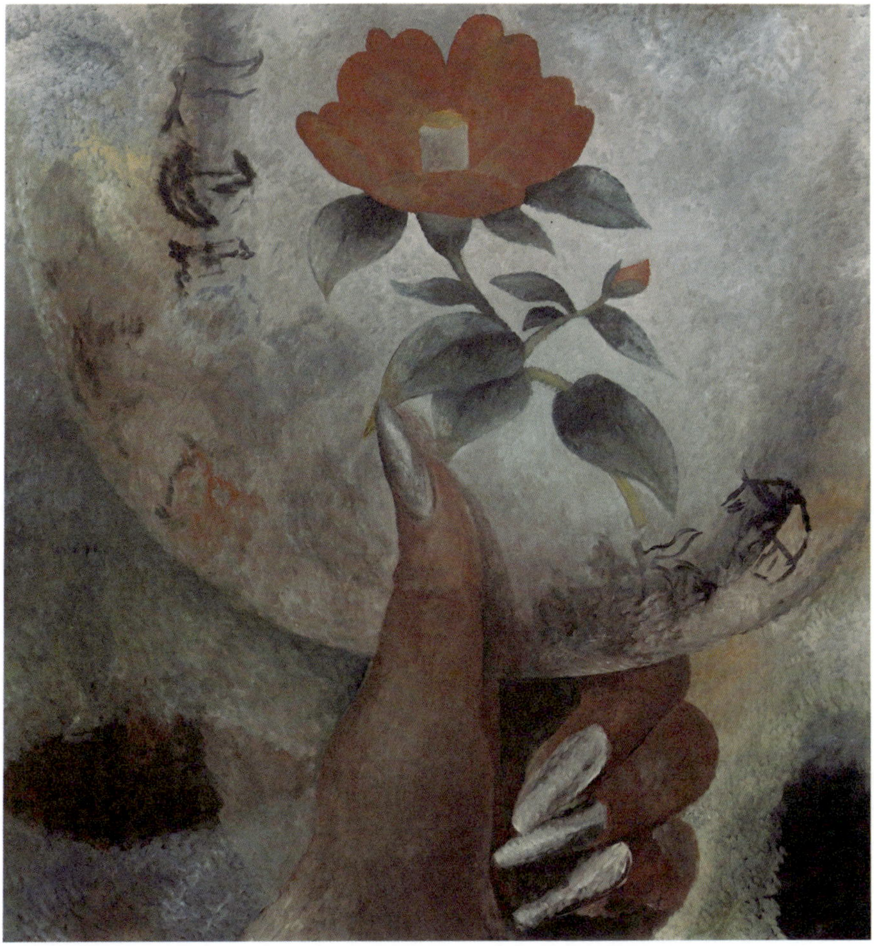

The Consultation
2017
Oil on canvas
228 x 206 cm

Claude Cahun

Claude Cahun (1894–1954) was born in Nantes, France, as Lucy Renée Mathilde Schwob, changing her name in 1919 after settling in Paris with her partner Marcel Moore. In the 1920s, Cahun began to create self-portraits in which she challenged traditional ideas of gender and identity. She became associated with the Surrealists in Paris in 1932, exhibiting with the group and contributing to its journals. Cahun settled in Jersey in 1937, where she and Moore fiercely resisted the German occupation during the Second World War.

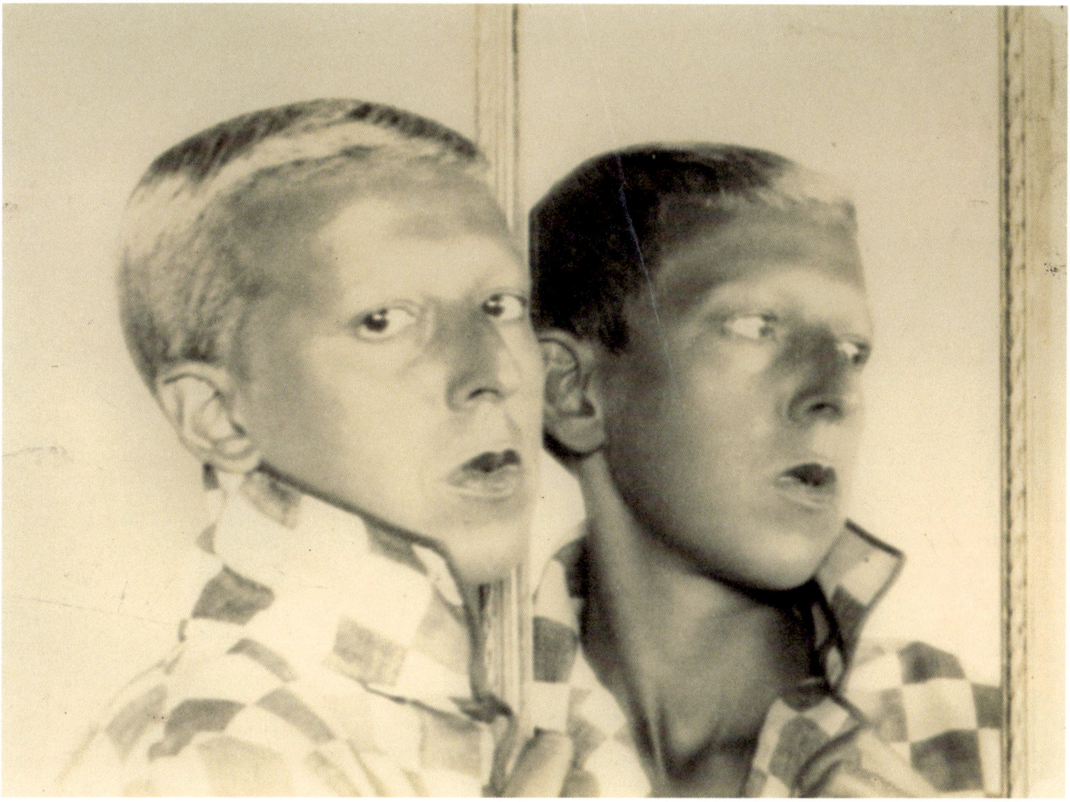

Self portrait (reflected in mirror)
1928
Gelatin silver print
17.9 x 23.7 cm

Gillian Wearing

Gillian Wearing was born 1963 in Birmingham. She lives and works in London. Recent solo exhibitions include Whitechapel Gallery, London (2012), touring to Düsseldorf and Munich; 'We Are Here', The New Art Gallery Walsall, UK (2013); Instituto Valenciano de Arte Moderno, Valencia, Spain (2015); and the Institute of Contemporary Art, Boston (2016). She has been commissioned to create the statue of suffragist leader Millicent Fawcett in Parliament Square, London, for 2018. Wearing won the Turner Prize in 1997 and was awarded an OBE in 2011.

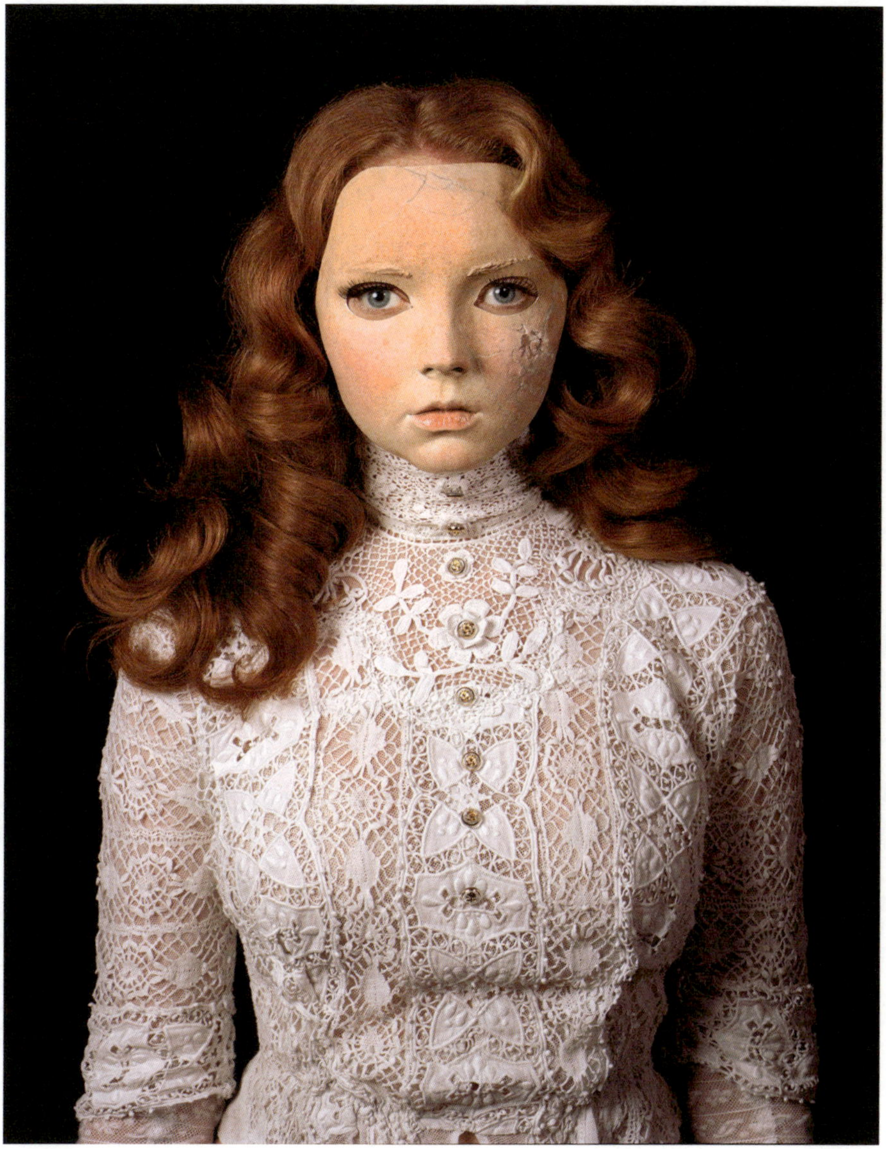

Lily Cole
2009
C-type colour photograph printed on Matt Fuji Crystal Archive paper
61 x 48 cm

‘To dress up, it is to change dimension, species, space. It is to be able to feel gigantic, to dive into vegetation, to become animal until one feels invulnerable and timeless, to meet, obscurely, in forgotten rituals. To dress up, to cross dress, is an act of creativity. And in applying this to oneself, one becomes other characters, or one’s proper character.’[17]

Surrealism cast women in symbolic roles: as priestess, muse, angel or harpy, and rather than shunning them, women Surrealists sometimes chose to adopt these multiple guises. The Argentinian Leonor Fini was a flamboyant figure who exhibited alongside the Surrealists, although not officially a member of the movement. The figures in her paintings all share her own feline features, making them a series of self-portraits with fluctuating details, reflecting multiplying 'selves' and so unmasking the idea of a single 'true' self as a masquerade.

The photographs from Francesca Woodman's brief, brilliant career feel like privately enacted performances in which she is both hiding and revealing herself. Her youth and elusive physicality have the potent charge the Surrealists fetishised in the *'femme-enfant'*, while her photographs have a haunting quality that is hard to disentangle from the tragedy of her early death. In dilapidated interiors, she blurs and disappears into her surroundings or fragments her body with reflections, while in nature she submerges in a pool or merges, clothed in bark, with a birch glade, like a nymph or dryad. There is a wilder, maenad quality to the secluded revels, sometimes in the company of other young women and animals, documented by Carina Brandes. Though involving little costume, the rites of both artists – enacting playfulness, vulnerability or power, shape-shifting into spirit, tree or beast – are an exploration of the malleability of the self through the trying-on of identities. Exulting in their youthful vigour, and emboldened by the dawning awareness of their sexuality, Donna Huddleston's 'warriors' are an athletic tribe of teenage suburban Amazons, forming a raiding party in visors and netball skirts. Like many of the Surrealist artists, they have animal familiars (as Carrington chose a horse, Tanning a dog, Remedios Varo an owl, Fini a cat): elegant hounds, more refined than Carrington's debutante's hyena friend.

One role of which the older generation of artists particularly were wary was that of 'woman artist'. In a culture privileging the masculine experience as universal, the female experience can be downgraded as local and partisan, and being a female artist is a perilous position. In seeking to redress the balance of attention, a woman-only show risks simultaneously reinforcing the definition of margin and centre. But this powerful, disparate, multifarious company of artists refutes a static definition of the 'other', offering pluralities over binaries. Rather than a static, monolithic masculine state of being, these artists represent identity as a state of continuous becoming. In Dorothea Tanning's kaleidoscopic work *Anges Mordus* (1962), bodies and limbs dissolve into one another and collapse towards abstraction; the negative space created by a male torso defines the form of a woman's back and bent head, while a beastly face materialises. Female identity appears as a place of porous boundaries and continual transformation and metamorphosis, containing multitudes. As Carrington fantasises in her 1970 essay, in an echo of Agar's imagery; 'I find pleasure in imagining that I am some kind of seed that must split and germinate into something so unlike what I appear to be that I could not imagine in my wildest moment, but intensely convinced that once the split is complete the absolute Other will take over in this field of doubting multitude I call myself and take a step further in evolution.'[18]

17. Leonor Fini, 'Mes Théâtres', *Corps écrit*, 1984, p.31.
18. Carrington, ibid.

Leonor Fini

Leonor Fini (1907–96) was born in Buenos Aires to Italian and Argentine parents and was raised by her mother in Trieste. After moving to Paris in 1931, she became acquainted with the Surrealist group, in particular Max Ernst, with whom she first exhibited in New York in 1936. Since her death, Fini has been the subject of a number of retrospectives, including Revoltella Museum, Trieste (2009); CFM Gallery, New York (2010); and Bildmuseet, Umeå, Sweden (2014).

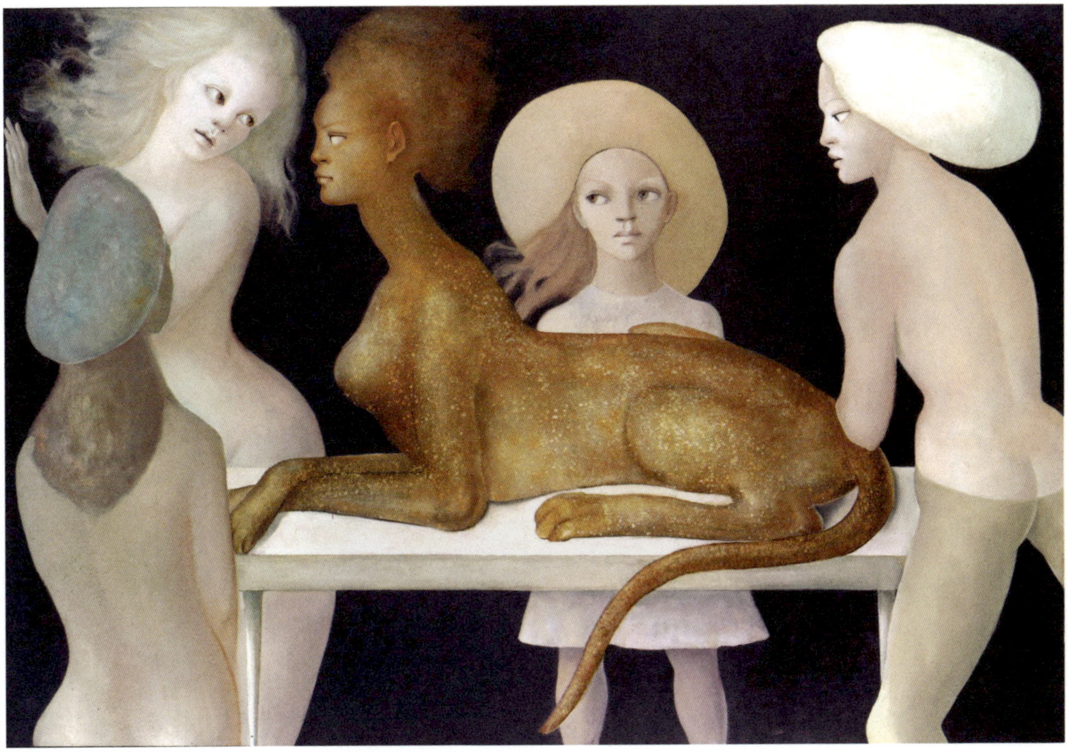

Lointaine parente
1970
Oil on canvas

Francesca Woodman

Francesca Woodman (1958–81) was born in Denver, Colorado, and lived in New York and Italy. Since her death, her work has been the subject of numerous solo presentations, including Fondation Cartier pour l'Art Contemporain, Paris (1998), touring to Rotterdam; The Photographers' Gallery, London (1999); San Francisco Museum of Modern Art (2011), touring to New York (2012); and 'On Being an Angel', Moderna Museet, Stockholm (2015), touring to Amsterdam, Paris, Malmo and Helsinki.

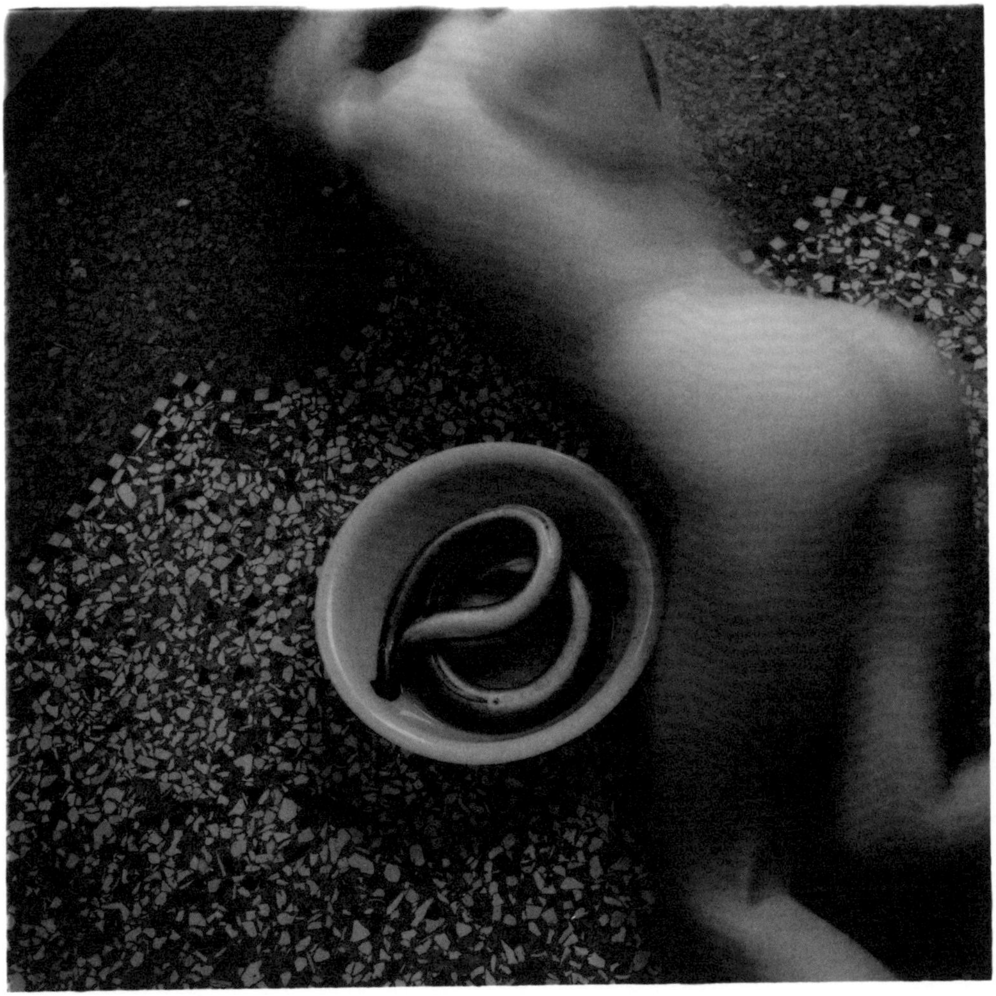

From Eel Series, Venice, Italy
1978
Gelatin silver estate print
27.9 x 35.6 cm

Carina Brandes

Carina Brandes was born in 1982 in Brunswick, Germany, and lives and works in Berlin. In her black-and-white photographs, Brandes is present as subject, exploring the fluid associations around the self in contemporary, often industrial, settings. In 2017, she was artist in residence at Villa Romana, Florence. Recent solo exhibitions include 'White Room', White Columns, New York (2012); 'Wilkommen', Team Gallery, New York (2014); and BQ, Berlin (2016). Group exhibitions include 'The Little Things Could Be Dearer', MoMA PS1, New York (2014); 'facing', Galerie Koal, Berlin (2016); and 'Produktion: Made in Germany Drei', Kunstverein Hannover (2017).

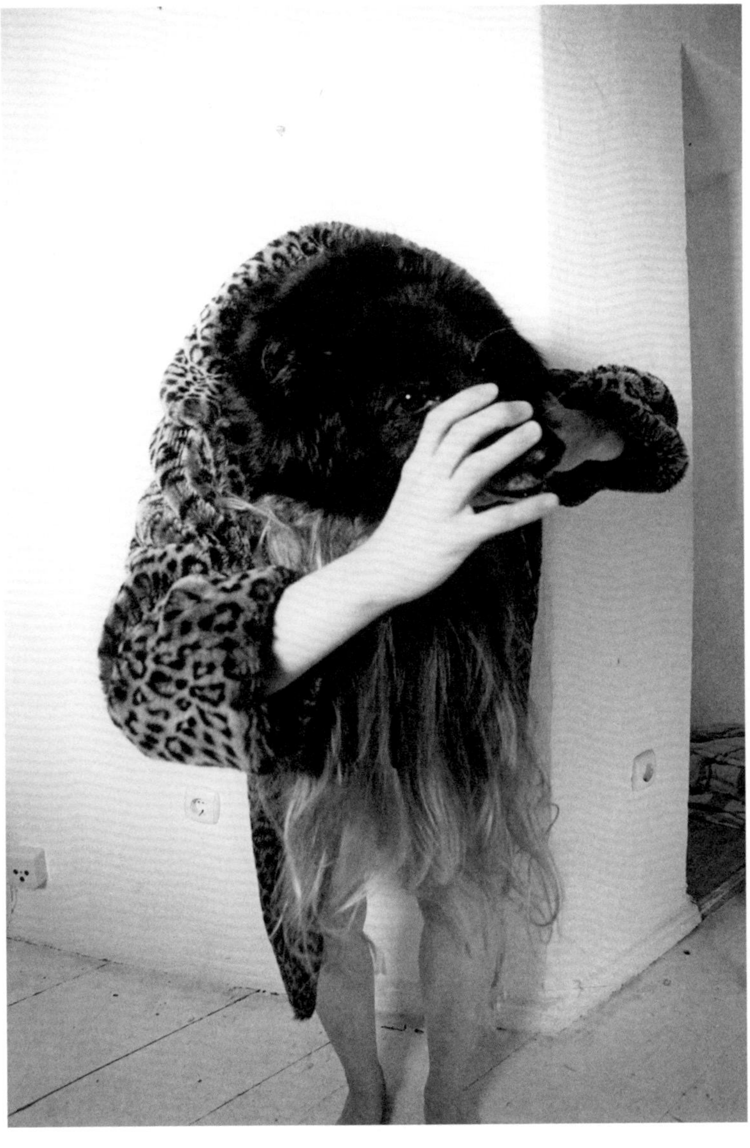

Untitled
2012
Black and white photograph on baryta
34.9 x 23.3 cm

Donna Huddleston

Donna Huddleston was born in 1970 in Belfast, grew up in Australia and lives and works in London. Recent solo exhibitions include 'Witch Dance' at Sadler's Wells, London (2012) and Drawing Room, London (2013). Huddleston participated in the group exhibitions 'Interstellar', Galerie Isabella Bortolozzi, Berlin (2015); 'Show Window', Kate MacGarry, London; 'One Day Something Happens: Paintings of People', Leeds Art Gallery; and 'Making and Unmaking', Camden Arts Centre, London (all 2016).

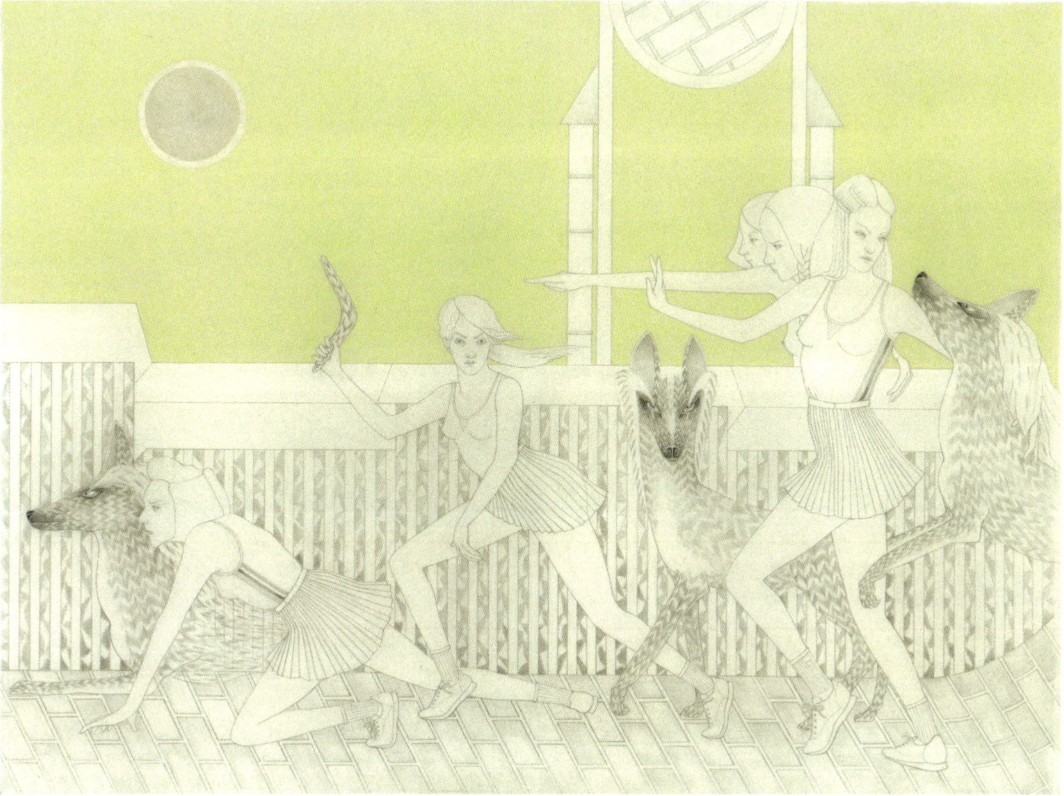

The Warriors in Fiji
2016
Graphite and Caran d'Ache on paper
46.5 x 62 cm

Dorothea Tanning

Dorothea Tanning (1910–2012) was born in Galesburg, Illinois. She attended art school in Chicago before moving to New York in the 1930s. Through her involvement in Peggy Guggenheim's seminal 'Exhibition by 31 Women' (1943) she was introduced to the Surrealist movement in New York and, in 1947, she took part in the 'Exposition Internationale du Surréalisme' in Paris, organised by Andre Breton and Marcel Duchamp. Selected solo exhibitions include 'Works 1942–1993', Camden Arts Centre, London (1993); 'Birthday and Beyond', Philadelphia Museum of Art (2000); and 'Night Shadows', Alison Jacques Gallery, London (2017).

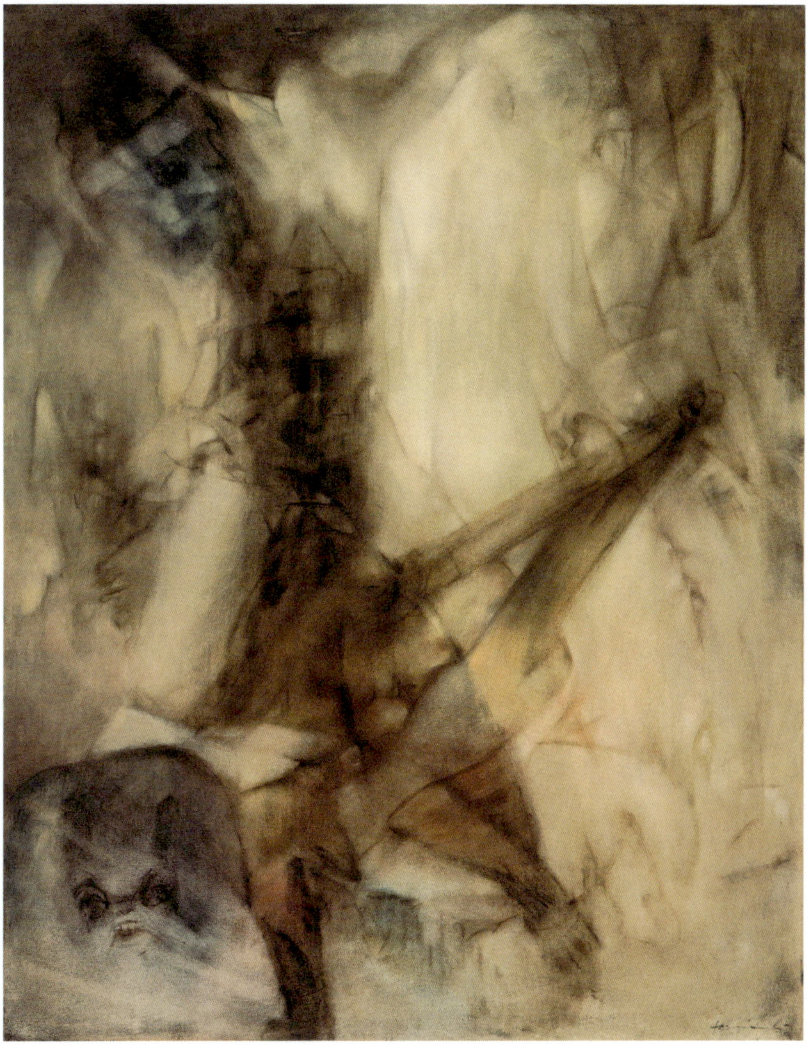

Anges Mordus (Anges Mordus par des Singes)
1962
Oil on linen
116.2 x 89.2 cm

P. 3
René Magritte
© ADAGP, Paris and DACS, London 2017. Courtesy of Bibliotheque Litteraire Jacques Doucet, Paris, France / Archives Charmet / Bridgeman Images

P. 4
Dorothea Tanning
© ADAGP, Paris and DACS, London 2017. Courtesy of the Philadelphia Museum of Art and Art Resource / Scala, Florence

P. 5
Leonor Fini
© ADAGP, Paris and DACS, London 2017. Courtesy ADAGP, Paris and Scala, Florence

P. 6
Kiki Smith
© the artist. Courtesy Timothy Taylor, London

P. 7
Mimi Parent
Courtesy of Musée national des beaux-arts du Québec. Photo: Jean-Guy Kérouac

P. 8
Frida Kahlo
© Banco de México Diego Rivera Frida Kahlo Museums Trust, Mexico, D.F. and DACS 2017. Courtesy of The Museum of Modern Art, New York and Scala, Florence

P. 9
Claude Cahun
Courtesy of the Jersey Heritage Collections

P. 10
Gillian Wearing
© Gillian Wearing. Courtesy Maureen Paley, London

P. 11
Francesca Woodman
© Betty Woodman. Courtesy Betty Woodman and Victoria Miro, London

P. 12
Jo Ann Callis
© Jo Ann Callis. Courtesy of the artist and ROSEGALLERY

P. 13
Hans Bellmer
Ubu Gallery, New York
© ADAGP, Paris and DACS, London 2017

P. 14
René Magritte
© ADAGP, Paris and DACS, London 2017. Courtesy of the Menil Collection, Houston and Bridgeman Images, London

P. 21
Shannon Bool
© The artist. Courtesy the artist and Daniel Faria Gallery

P. 23
Kiki Smith
© The artist. Courtesy Pace Gallery

P. 25
Caitlin Keogh
© The artist. Courtesy of the artist and Bortolami, New York

P. 27
Louise Bourgeois & Tracey Emin
© The Easton Foundation / VAGA, New York; DACS, London 2017 and © Tracey Emin. Courtesy Carolina Nitsch Contemporary Art and Hauser & Wirth

P. 29
Jo Ann Callis
© The artist. Courtesy of the artist and ROSEGALLERY

P. 31
Penny Slinger
© The artist. Courtesy Riflemaker London Ltd

P. 35
Mona Hatoum
© The artist. Courtesy the artist and White Cube. Photo © Edward Woodman, courtesy White Cube

P. 37
Helen Chadwick
© The Estate of Helen Chadwick. Courtesy Richard Saltoun Gallery. Photo: Karen Bengall

P. 39
Nevine Mahmoud
© The artist. Courtesy of M+B. Photo: Jeff McLane

P. 41
Sarah Lucas
© Sarah Lucas. Courtesy Sadie Coles HQ, London

P. 43
Alina Szapocznikow
© ADAGP, Paris. Courtesy The Estate of Alina Szapocznikow / Piotr Stanislawski / Galerie Loevenbruck, Paris. Photo: Fabrice Gousset

P. 45
Julia Phillips
© The artist. Courtesy the artist and Campoli Presti, London / Paris

P. 47
Edith Rimmington
© The artist's estate. Courtesy the Murray Family Collection

P. 49
Linder
© The artist. Courtesy Stuart Shave / Modern Art, London. Photo: Robert Glowacki

P. 51
Laurie Simmons
© The artist. Courtesy the artist and Salon 94, New York

P. 53
Lee Miller
© Lee Miller Archives, England 2017. All rights reserved

P. 55
Shana Moulton
© The artist. Courtesy of Galerie Crèvecoeur, Paris and Galerie Gregor Staiger, Zürich

P. 57
A K Dolven
© The artist. Courtesy Wilkinson Gallery, London

P. 59
Julie Curtiss
© The artist. Courtesy the artist

P. 63
Rosemarie Trockel
© The artist and DACS, 2017. Courtesy Private Collection

P. 65
Kelly Akashi
© The artist. Courtesy the artist and Ghebaly Gallery, Los Angeles. Photo: Jeff McLane

P. 67
Berlinde De Bruyckere
© The artist. Courtesy the artist and Private Collection, London

P. 69
Hayv Kahraman
© The artist. Courtesy the artist and Jack Shainman Gallery, New York

P. 71
Rachel Kneebone
© The artist. Courtesy the artist and White Cube. Photo © Stephen White, courtesy White Cube

P. 73
Louise Bourgeois
© The Easton Foundation/VAGA, New York and DACS, London 2017. Courtesy Hauser & Wirth

P. 77
Hannah Wilke
© Hannah Wilke Collection & Archive, Los Angeles. Courtesy Alison Jacques Gallery, London and Hannah Wilke Collection and Archive, Los Angeles

P. 79
Maria Bartuszová
© The Archive of Maria Bartuszová. Courtesy The Estate of Maria Bartuszová, Košice and Alison Jacques Gallery, London

P. 81
Siobhán Hapaska
© The artist. Courtesy the artist and Kerlin Gallery, Dublin. Photo: Denis Mortell

P. 83
Ithell Colquhoun
© The artist. Courtesy The Sherwin Collection, Leeds and Bridgeman Images

P. 85
Loie Hollowell
© The artist. Courtesy the artist and Feuer / Mesler Gallery

P. 89
Eileen Agar
© Artist's Estate. Courtesy Private Collection and Redfern Gallery, London

P. 91
Gabriella Boyd
© The artist. Courtesy the artist and Folio Society

P. 93
Grace Pailthorpe
© Artist's estate. Courtesy of Redfern Gallery, London

P. 95
Eva Kot'átková
© The artist. Courtesy the artist and Hunt Kastner, Prague

P. 97
Carol Rama
© Archivio Carol Rama, Torino. Photo: Pino Dell'Acquila, Torino

P. 99
Paloma Varga Weisz
© The artist. Courtesy Sadie Coles HQ, London. Photo: Stefan Hostettler, VG-Bild Kunst, Bonn

P. 101
Tomoko Kashiki
© The artist. Courtesy Ota Fine Arts, Tokyo / Singapore

P. 103
Sascha Braunig
© The artist. Courtesy Office Baroque, Brussels. Photo: Johan Blommaert

P. 105
Jordan Kasey
© The artist. Courtesy the artist and Nicelle Beauchene Gallery, New York

P. 107
Cheyenne Julien
© The artist. Courtesy the artist

P. 111
Leonora Carrington
© Estate of Leonora Carrington / ARS, NY and DACS, London 2017. Courtesy of the Metropolitan Museum of Art and Art Resource / Scala, Florence

P. 113
Elizabeth Jaeger
© The artist. Courtesy the artist and Jack Hanley Gallery

P. 115
Issy Wood
© The artist. Courtesy the artist and Carlos / Ishikawa, London

P. 117
Claude Cahun
Courtesy of the Jersey Heritage Collections

P. 119
Gillian Wearing
© The artist. Courtesy Maureen Paley, London

P. 123
Leonor Fini
© ADAGP, Paris and DACS, London 2017. Courtesy BI, ADAGP, Paris / Scala, Florence

P. 125
Francesca Woodman
© Betty Woodman. Courtesy Betty Woodman and Victoria Miro, London

P. 127
Carina Brandes
© The artist. Courtesy BQ, Berlin. Photo: Roman März, Berlin

P. 129
Donna Huddleston
© The artist. Courtesy the artist

P. 131
Dorothea Tanning
© ADAGP, Paris and DACS, London 2017. Courtesy Michael Rosenfeld Gallery